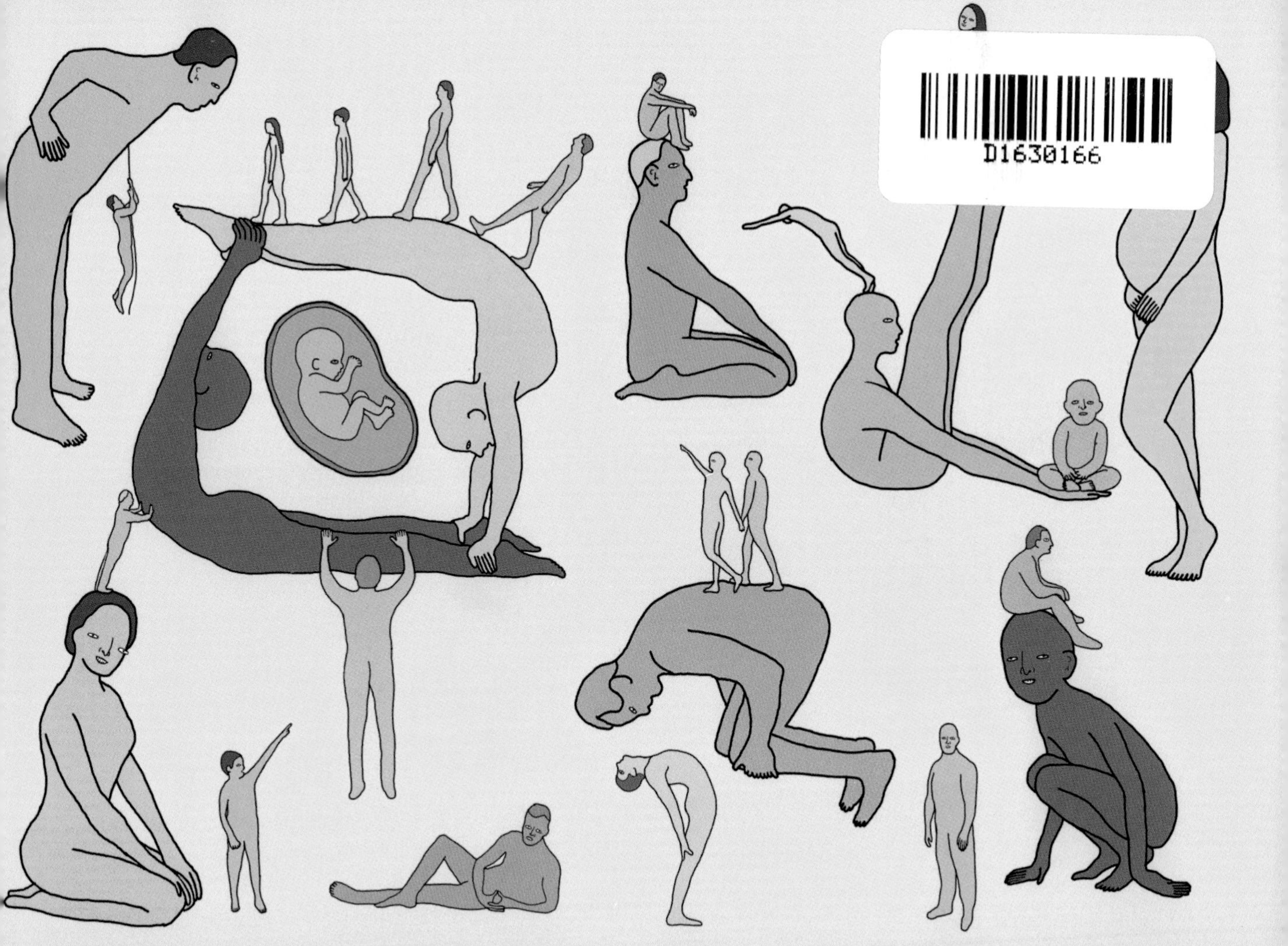

First published in Great Britain in 2017 by Trapeze
an imprint of The Orion Publishing Group Ltd
Carmelite House, 50 Victoria Embankment, London EC4Y 0DZ

An Hachette UK Company

1 3 5 7 9 10 8 6 4 2

A CIP catalogue record for this book is available from the British Library.

ISBN 978 1 409 17584 1

ISBN (eBook) 978 1 409 17585 8

Printed in Italy

MIX
Paper from responsible sources
FSC® C023419

www.orionbooks.co.uk

the story of life

by chris (simpsons artist)

for
all of my friends
and my mum
xox

introduction

hello and welcome to my book
inside of these pages you will be taken on a magical journey through life
i hope that you will enjoy having a read of it and if you cant read
then i hope that you have a nice time touching and sniffing all of the pages
and looking at all of the pictures

love from your friend
Chris (Simpsons artist) xox

warning: i told everyone that my last book was completely edible when it actually wasnt
and quite a lot of people sadly died from having a eat of it so i have been asked to put a warning
inside of this book to tell you that you cant eat it because there is a chance that you will die
i am sorry to all of the people who ate my last book i didnt mean for there to be so much death

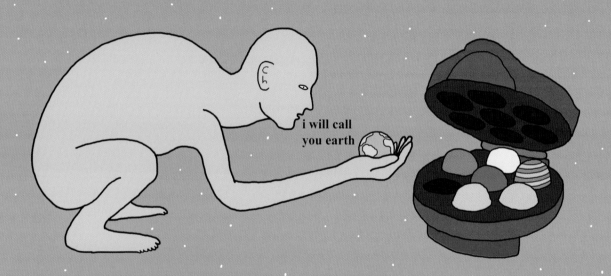

the planets and everything that we know was made by the creator whos name was called leaf
he cherished every single planet like they was his son but earth was his favourite planet
of them all so he decided to give it life and that is why we are all here today

the first humans were invented by fish nearly two thousand years ago when they
decided to grow human legs because they were fed up of being in the sea
because there was nothing exciting for them in the water anymore
so they came onto land to try
and find something
else to do

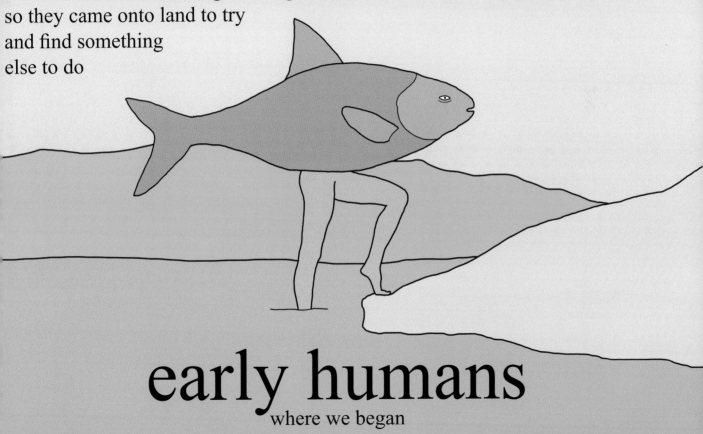

early humans
where we began

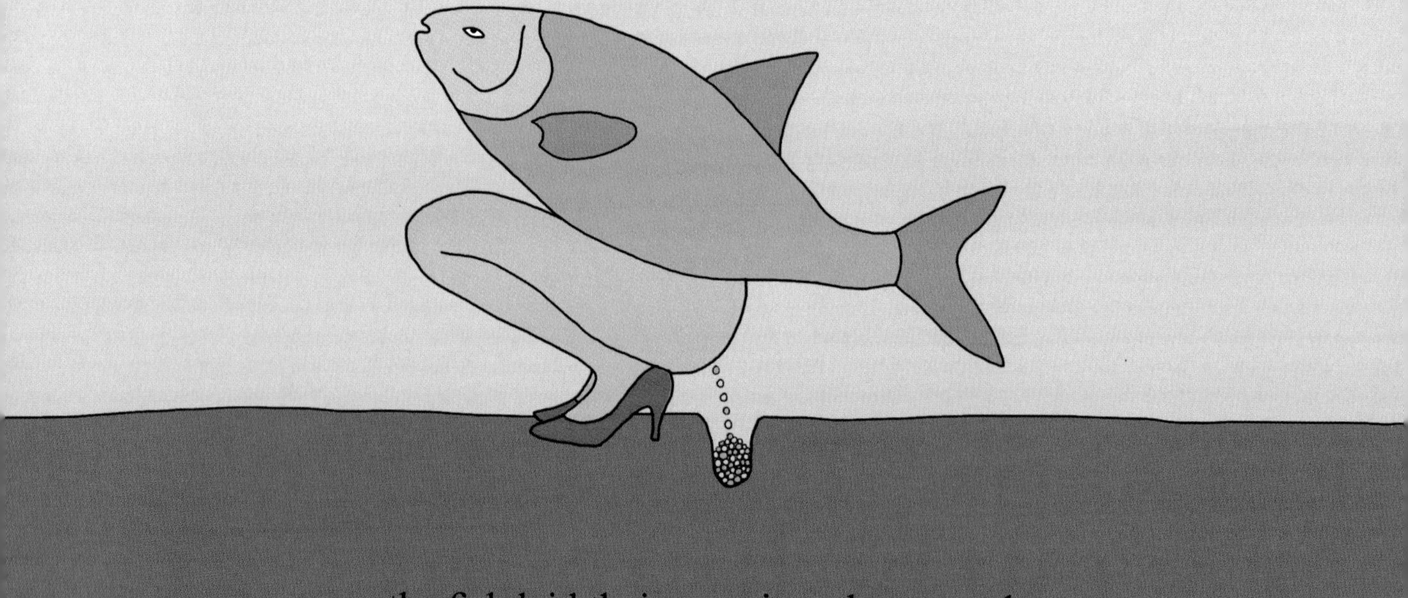

the fish laid their eggs into the ground

and the eggs growed into the first humans

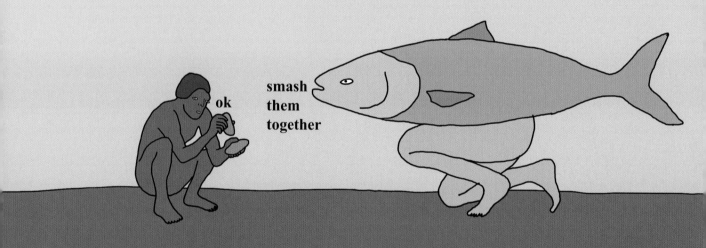

we lived alongside the fish for many years
they took care of us and they showed us the secrets of the earth

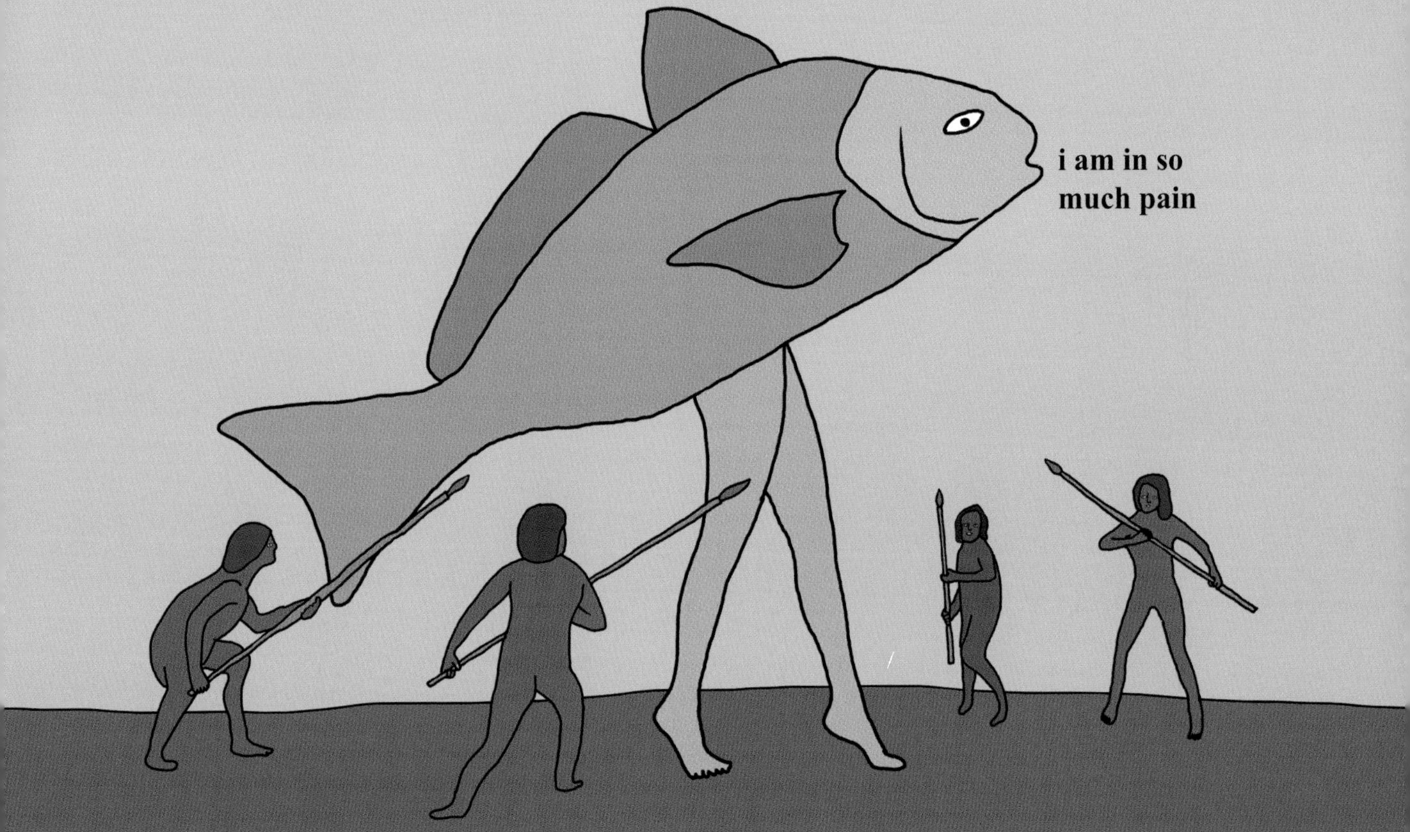
i am in so
much pain

but then we got hungry and greedy and we hunted all of the fish until there
was no fish left on the land and humans was now the main creatures of the earth

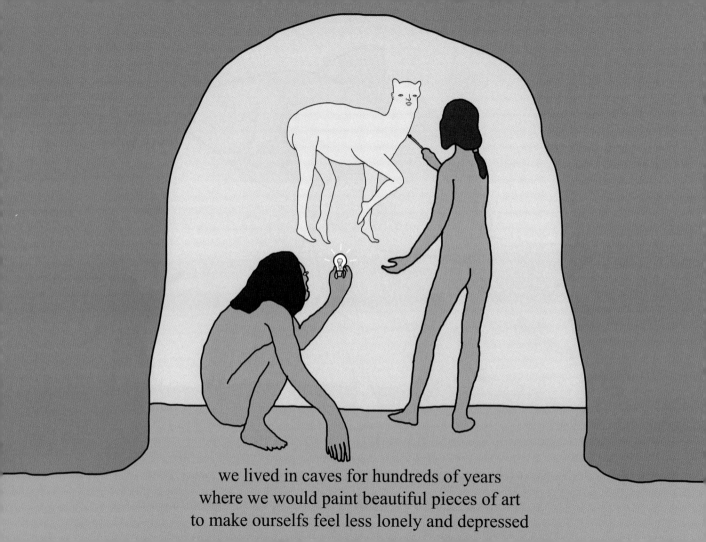

we lived in caves for hundreds of years
where we would paint beautiful pieces of art
to make ourselfs feel less lonely and depressed

<u>fact of life</u>

**the oldest human nose ever discovered
was nearly 175 years old
wow now that is a old nose**

but then 600 years ago something magical happened
and the shoe was invented and modern man was born

thanks to shoes people could now walk further and further
without getting sore feet and that is why today we live all over the earth
and this is the story of all of our lives

before birth

grow my child for you are the new beginning

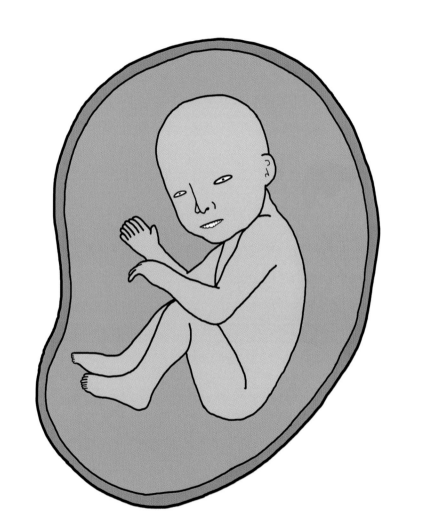

the miracle of life

nowadays there are lots of ways a lady can get pregnant
but the most popular way is for a man to lay a egg into a ladys mouth
so she can swallow it inside of herself and grow it into a baby

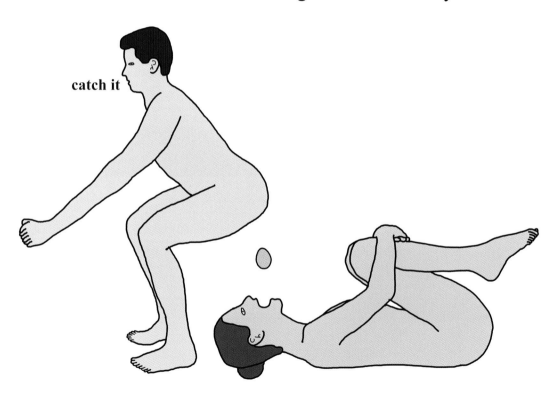

catch it

how big is the baby inside of the lady

4 weeks - the baby is now the size of a mans nose

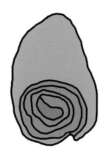

10 weeks - the baby is now about the size of a pair of rolled up boot cut mens leggings

20 weeks - the baby is now the size of a cheese and ham omelette

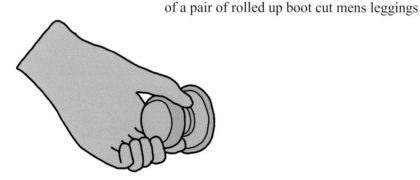

25 weeks - the baby is now the size of a hand opening a door

30 weeks - the baby is now the size of the pop rap singer drakes face

the swelling of the feet

womens feet swell up to eleven times the normal size
when they are pregnant this is because the placenta[1]
is grown and stored inside of the feet

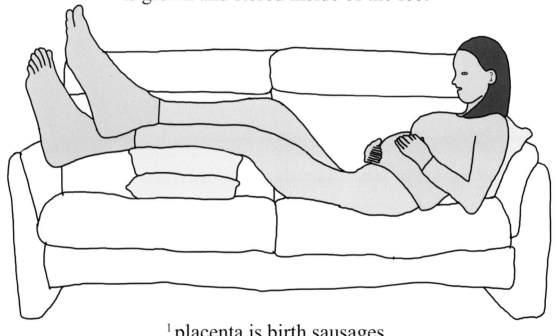

[1] placenta is birth sausages

when a lady has 2 babies inside of her it is called
being pregnant with twins

the reason most people have got 2 legs is incase they get
pregnant with twins so that they can safely grow them
inside of their legs with plenty of room

the twins will feed on the leg bone of
their mother to get all of the bone goodness
that is needed to help them grow

by the time the twins are fully grown they will have
stretched all of the way down to their mothers ankles

what a beautiful world we live in

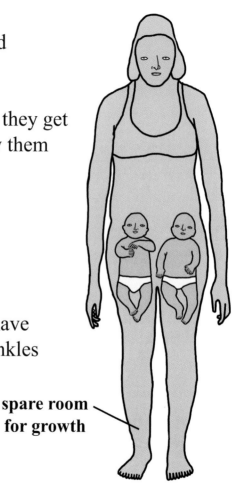

**spare room
for growth**

after thirty weeks of being pregnant
the baby is now fully formed inside
of the ladys body and it will soon
be time for the birthing

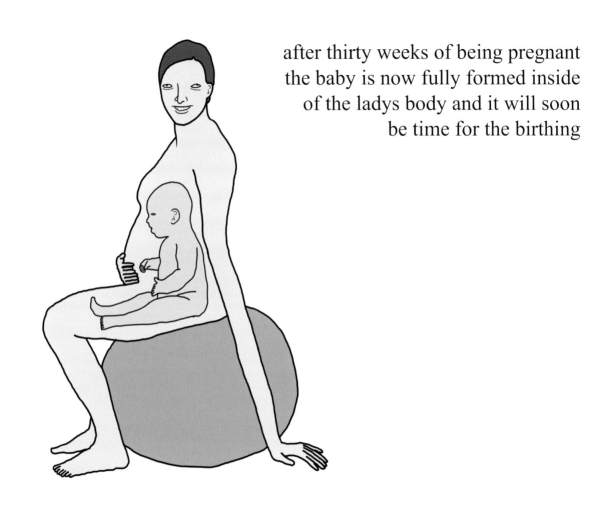

fact of life

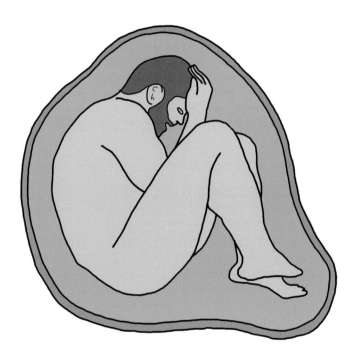

the longest known pregnancy was 32 years and 11 days
when the man was asked why he stayed in the womb for so long
he just said he couldnt be bothered being born

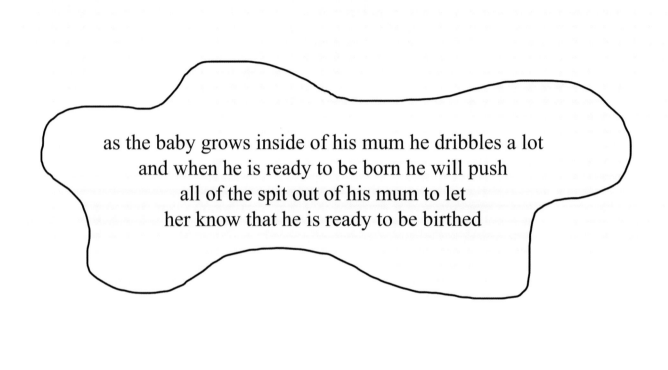

as the baby grows inside of his mum he dribbles a lot
and when he is ready to be born he will push
all of the spit out of his mum to let
her know that he is ready to be birthed

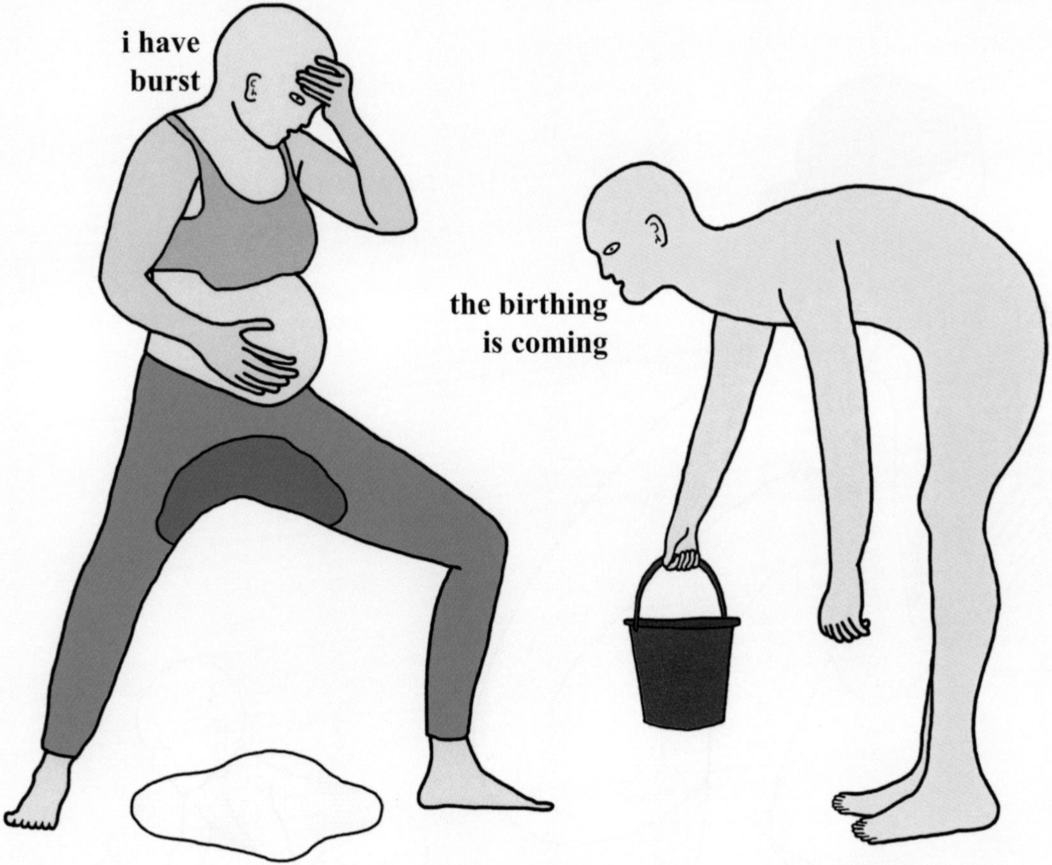
i have burst
the birthing is coming

the birthing - welcome to the world

when the baby is ready to be born
the woman will crouch down and
let the newborn crawl out of her
so it can finally be released
into the wild

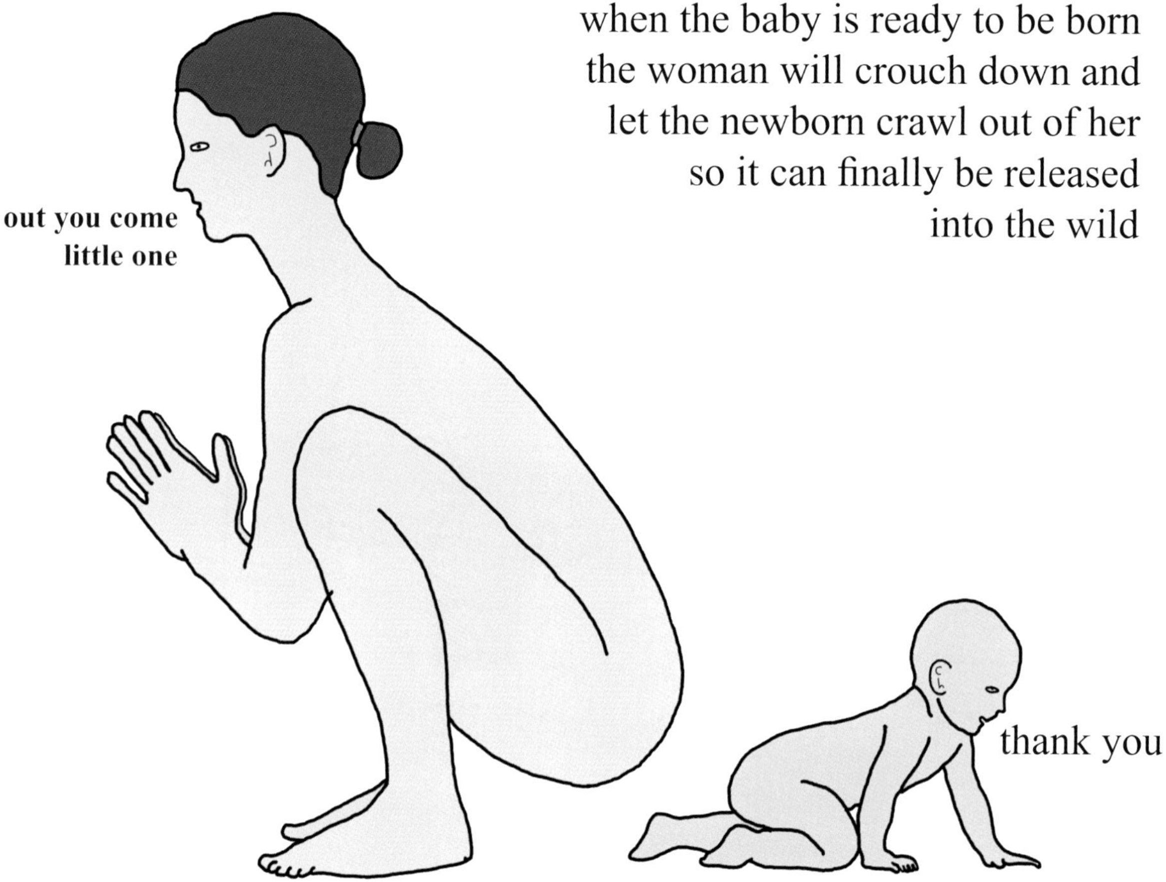

out you come
little one
thank you

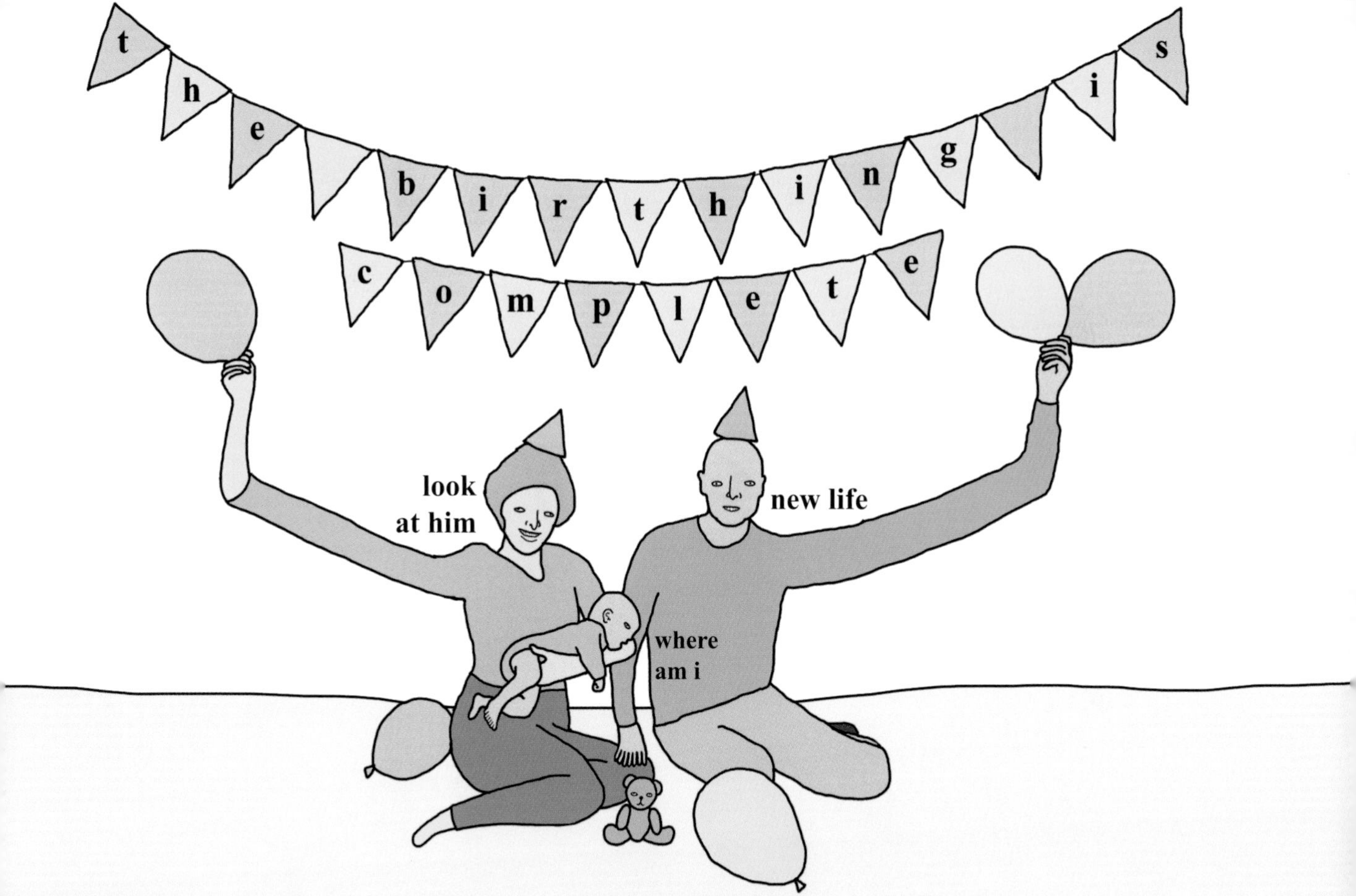

t h e b i r t h i n g i s
c o m p l e t e
look at him
new life
where am i

a new life has begun

baby
you are born

the inside of a babys mind

nipple juice
sleeps
darkness
why
am i real
where
am i

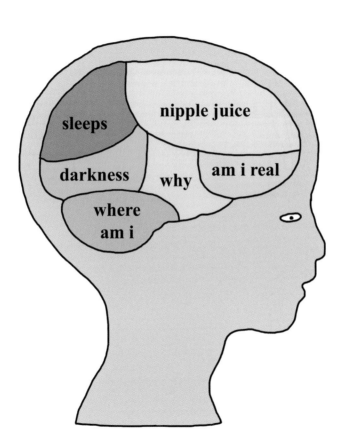

babies grow very quickly

1 week old

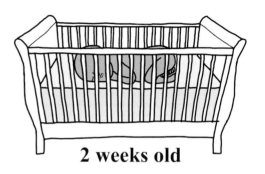

2 weeks old

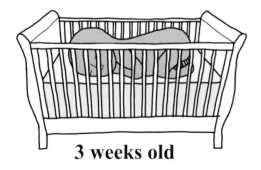

3 weeks old

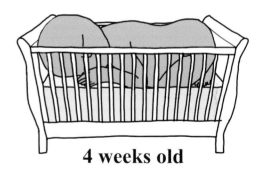

4 weeks old

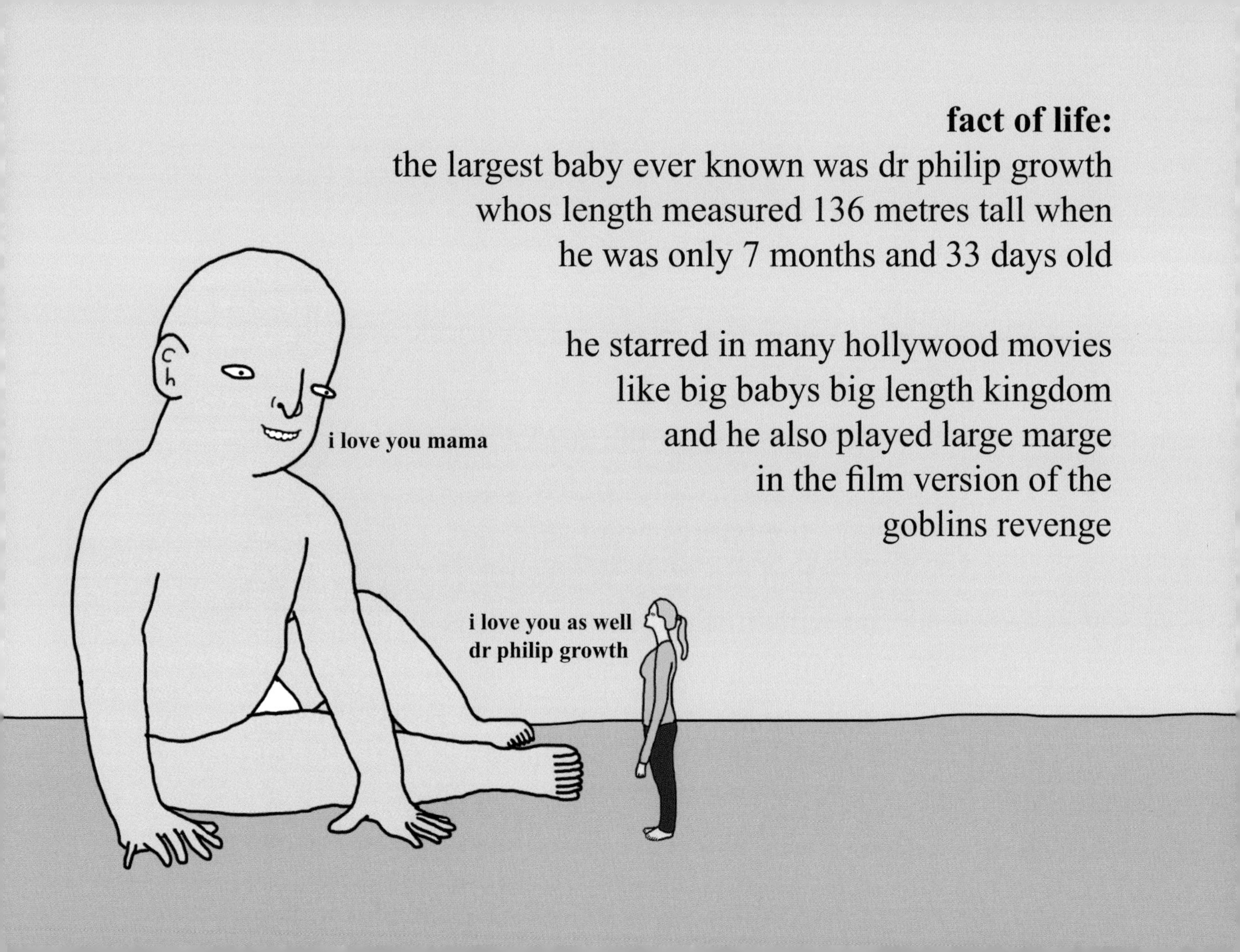

fact of life:
the largest baby ever known was dr philip growth
whos length measured 136 metres tall when
he was only 7 months and 33 days old

he starred in many hollywood movies
like big babys big length kingdom
and he also played large marge
in the film version of the
goblins revenge

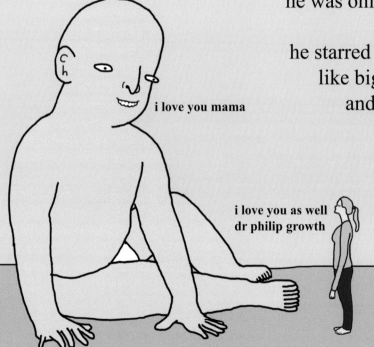

i love you mama

i love you as well
dr philip growth

beware of the stork
say the ladies in town
the babies arent safe
when the stork is around
he will sniff out the newborns
with his long orange nose
to keep in his nest
with the others he chose

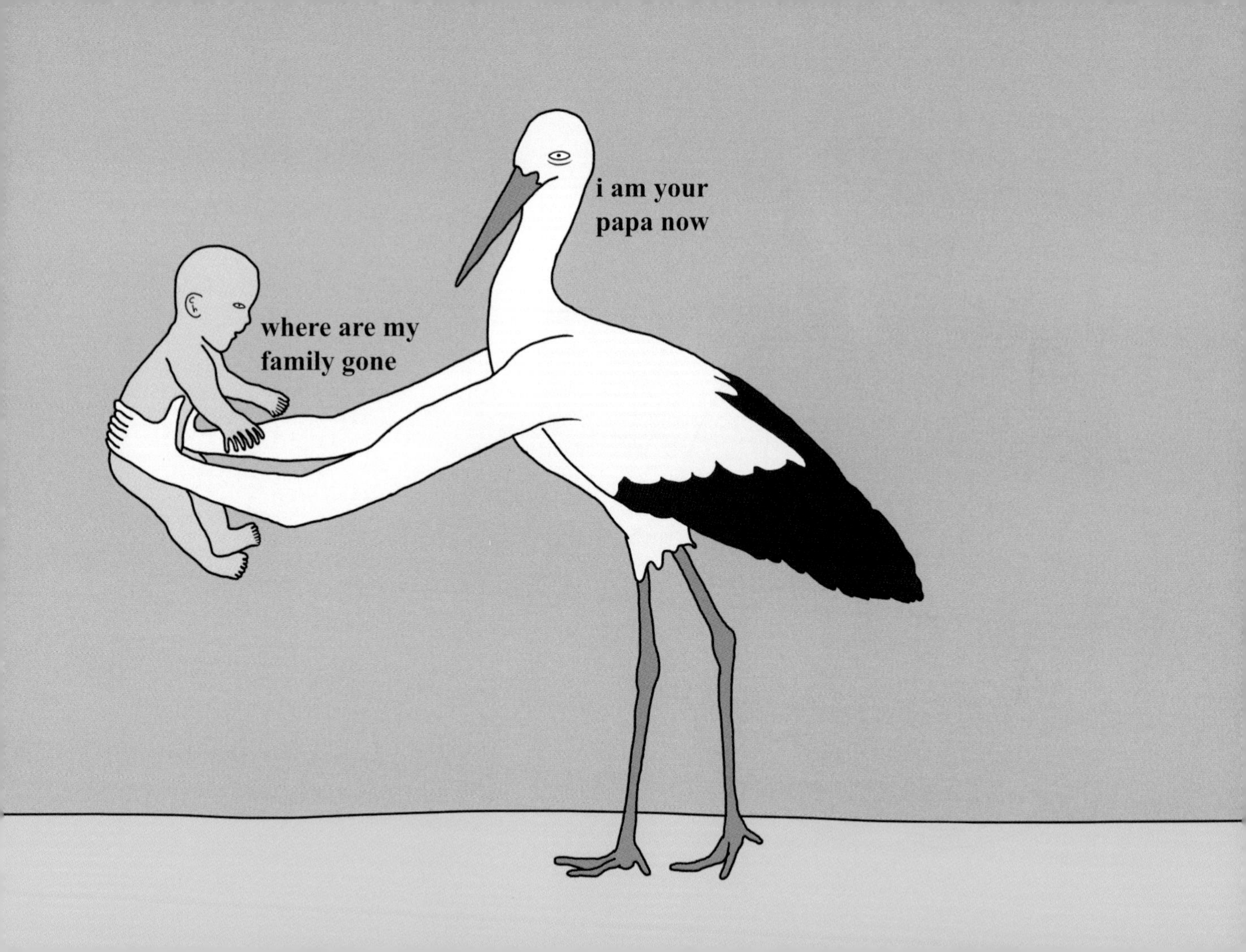
i am your
papa now
where are my
family gone

age 1 month - feeding time

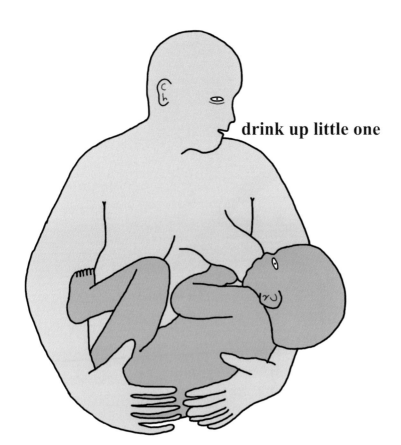

drink up little one

feeding time is a natural way
for babies to bond with papa

first words

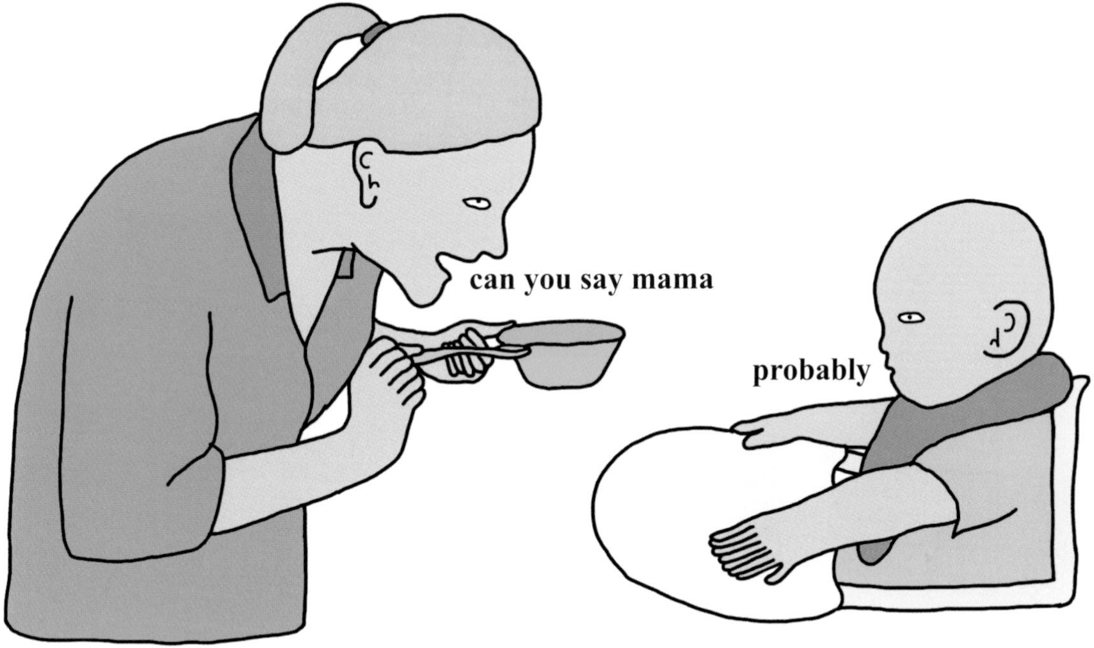
can you say mama
probably

a baby will say its first words at 8 days old
by the time that they are 10 weeks old they can
speak as well as a full grown man

a popular nursery rhyme
to soothe babies to sleep:
humpty dumpty

life is perfect

humpty dumpty sat on a wall
humpty dumpty had a great fall

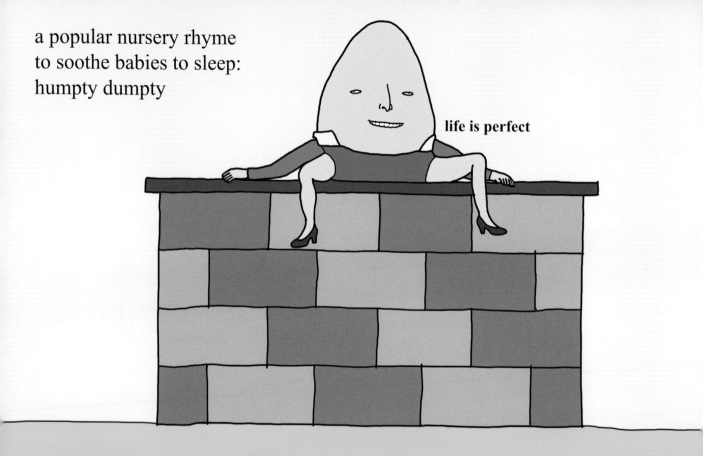

all the kings horses and all the kings men
spooned out his mind
and then they ate him

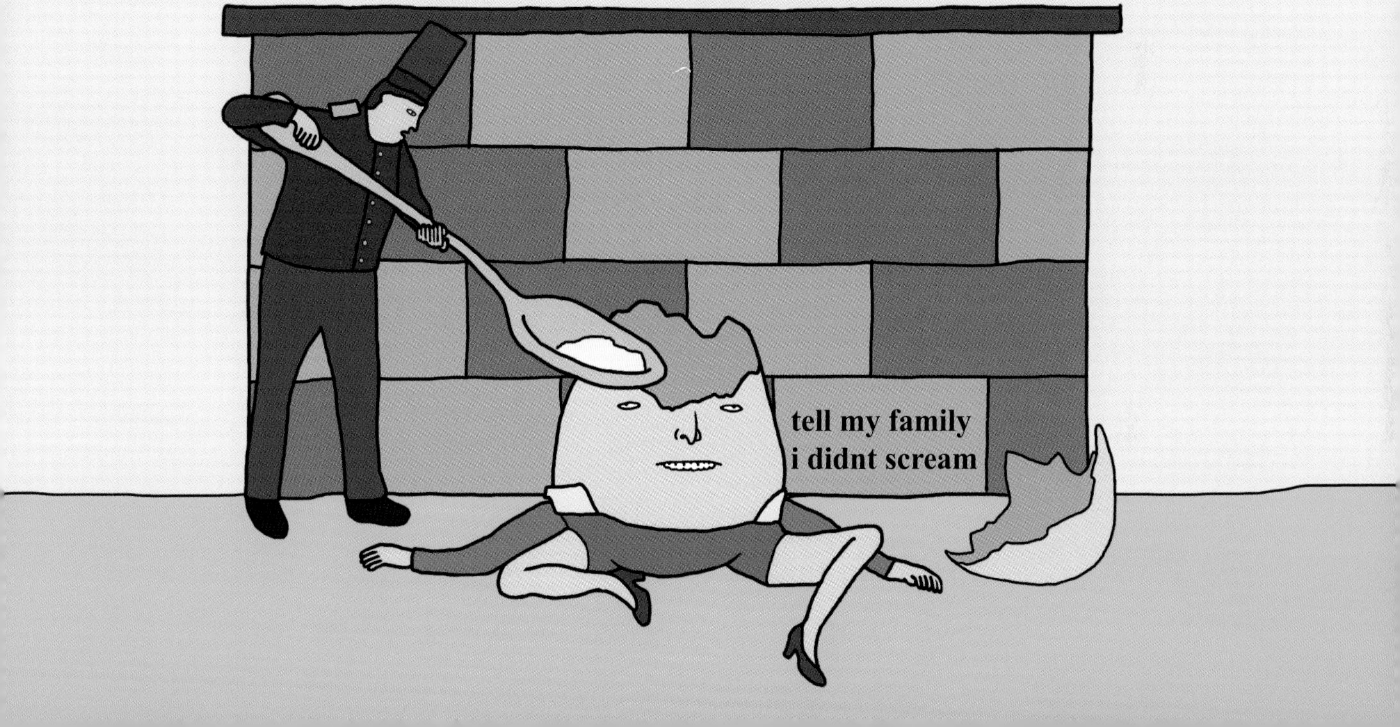
tell my family
i didnt scream

spit blessings
my sweet child

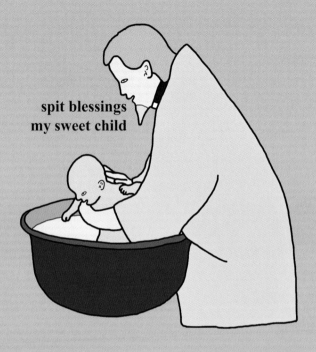

just before a babys 1st birthday the local priest will
bless the baby in a cauldron of priest spit
to protect the youngling from bad spirits

becoming a child

when a baby gets to about 2 years old
they will shed their baby legs and grow their child legs
this is known as the first step of becoming a child
it is a tradition to leave your childrens baby legs
under their pillow to be collected by the leg fairy
in exchange for £100 - £350 per leg

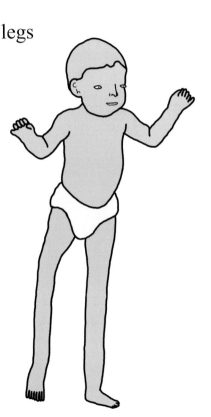

child

a child is a small human

the inside of a childs body

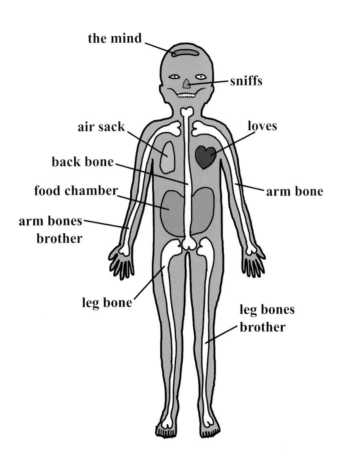

the mind

sniffs

air sack

loves

back bone

food chamber

arm bone

arm bones
brother

leg bone

leg bones
brother

food

children love the taste of food
it helps them be strong and healthy
but if they dont eat enough of it
they will shrivel up and die

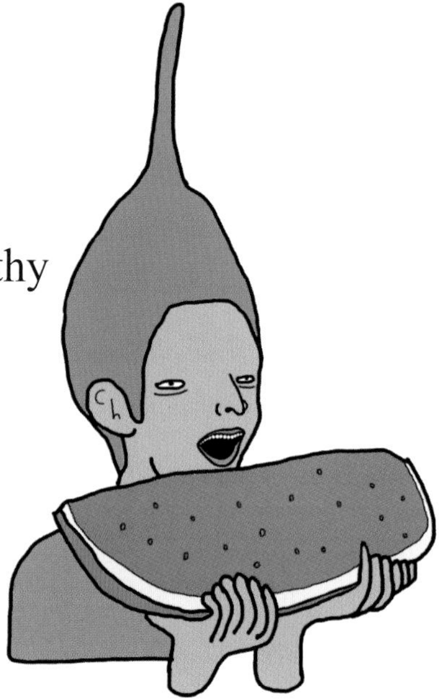

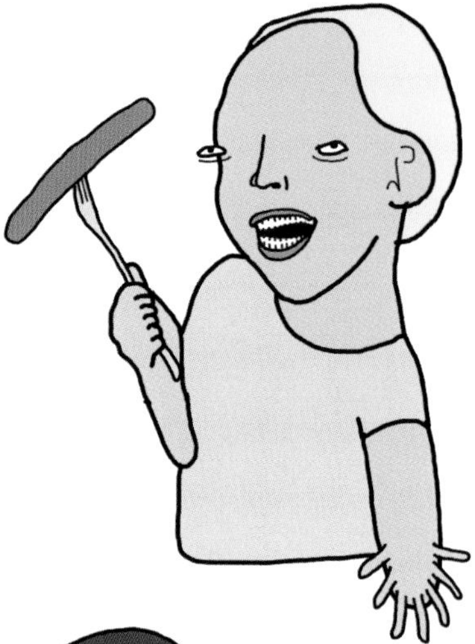

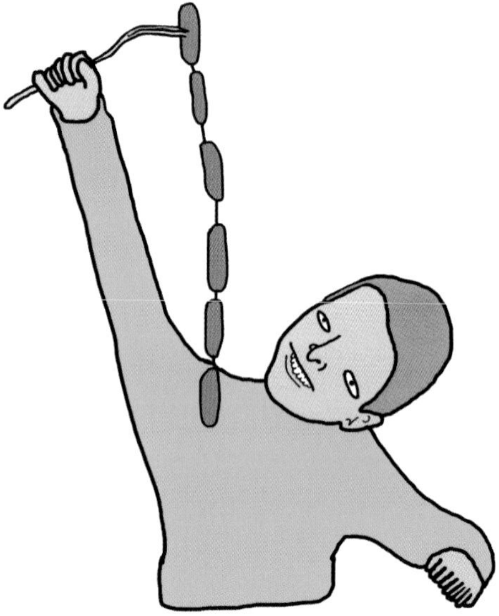

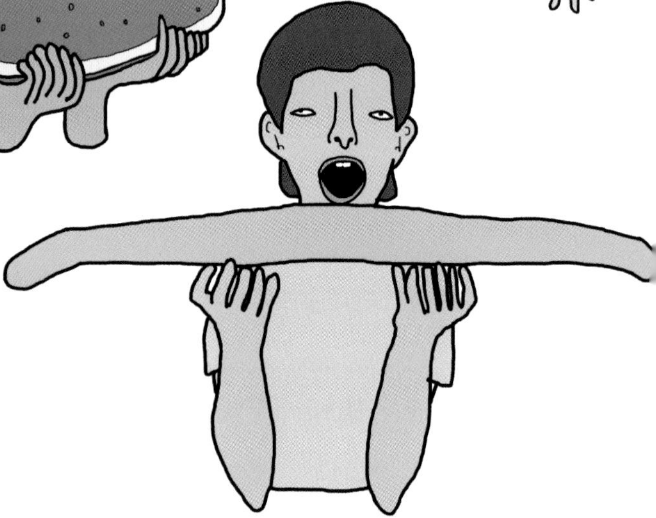

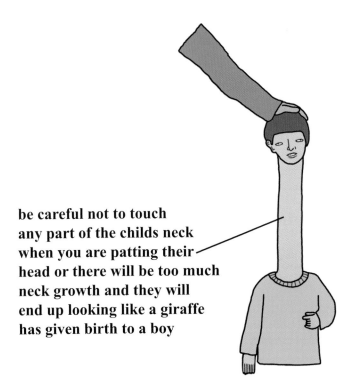

be careful not to touch
any part of the childs neck
when you are patting their
head or there will be too much
neck growth and they will
end up looking like a giraffe
has given birth to a boy

everytime a child is patted on their head they get taller
a child whos head is not patted will not get taller
that is why it is important to always have a pat
of a childs head even if they have horrible hair

learning

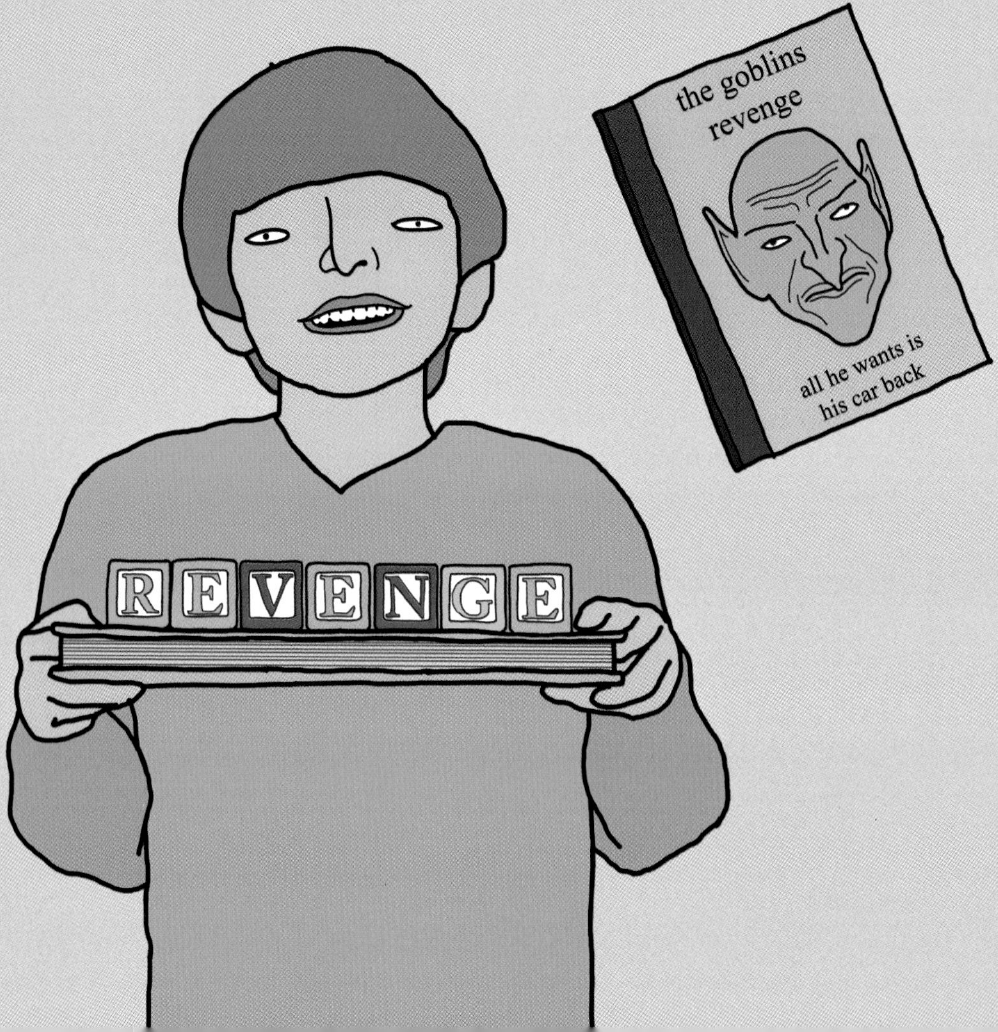
the goblins
revenge
all he wants is
his car back
REVENGE

children start being able to gulp up the learns when they are 5 years old and most children get their learns from books the most popular childrens book in the world is called the goblins revenge and it is about a goblin who goes completely mental when he finds out his car has been stolen when he parked it overnight in the Tesco car park at the retail park because he was too tired to drive it home and my best bit in the whole of the book is when the goblin runs into Tesco and he starts knocking loads of things off the shelves with his face because he is so angry that his car has been stolen and then right at the end of the book he strangles the manager of Tesco with a pipe that he pulls off one of the walls in the staffroom.

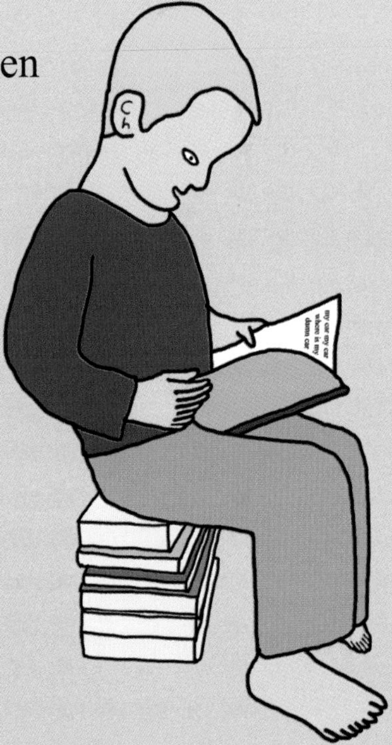
my car my car
where is my
damn car

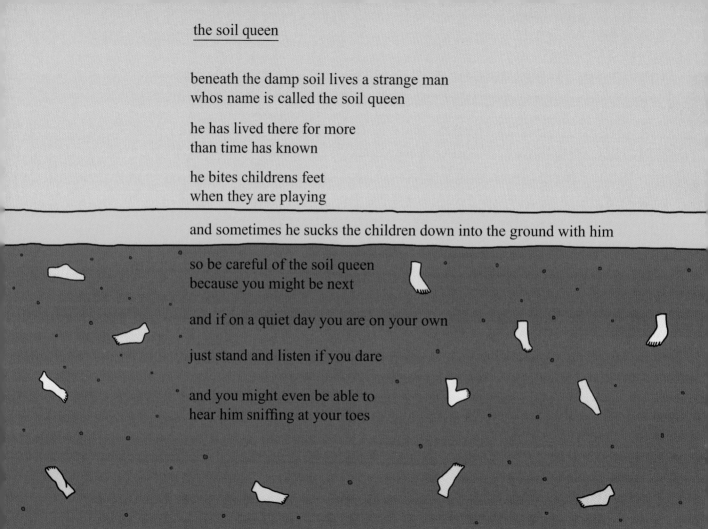

the soil queen

beneath the damp soil lives a strange man
whos name is called the soil queen

he has lived there for more
than time has known

he bites childrens feet
when they are playing

and sometimes he sucks the children down into the ground with him

so be careful of the soil queen
because you might be next

and if on a quiet day you are on your own

just stand and listen if you dare

and you might even be able to
hear him sniffing at your toes

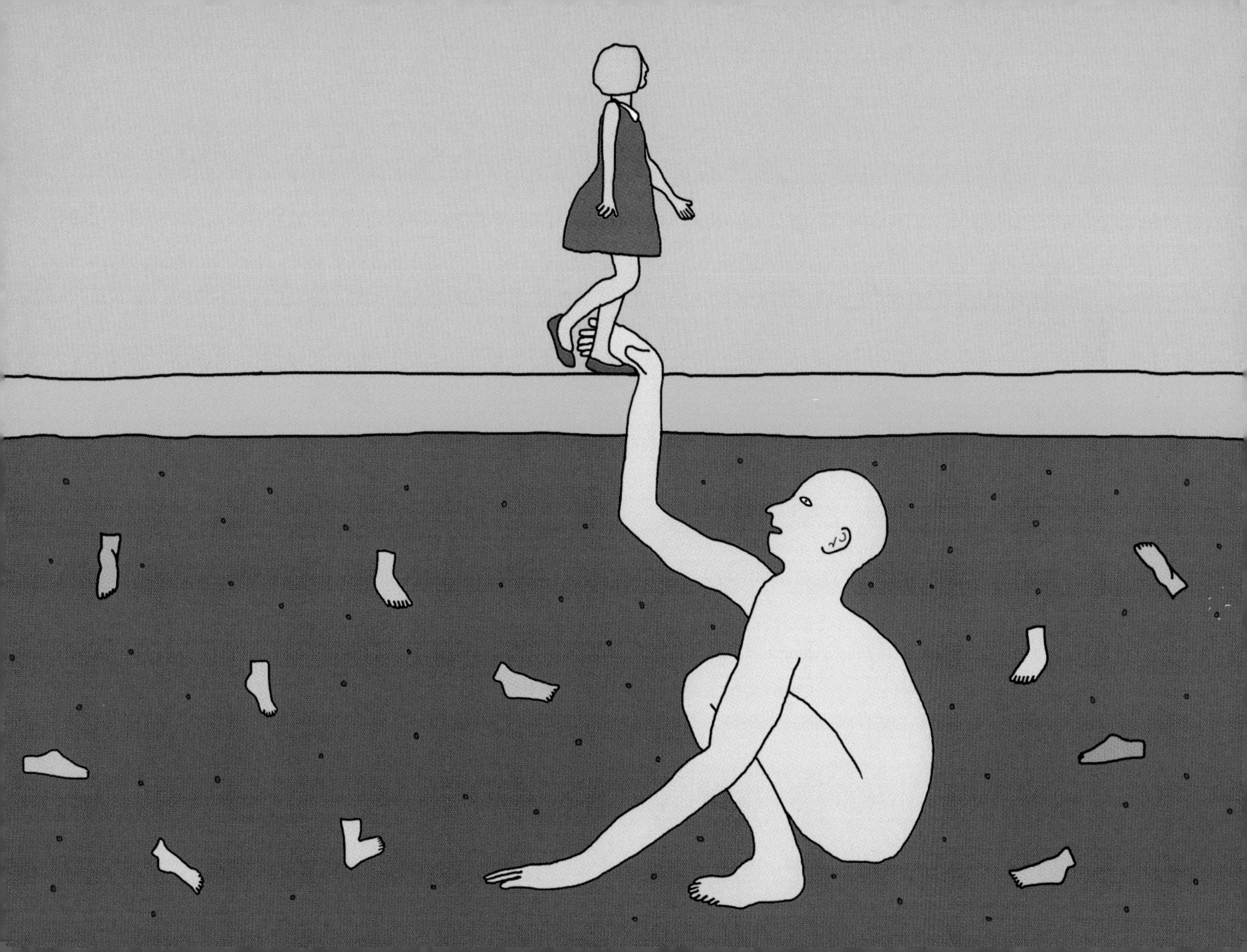

children love to play games it is their main thing that they like to do
a popular childrens game is called pass the baguette

in this game a group of children all gather round in a circle and they have to pass a baguette around the circle while a man whistles the song here comes the bride and when the man shouts whos got my baguette the child holding the baguette has to eat it as quickly as they can before the man can wrestle it out of their hands and eat it for himself

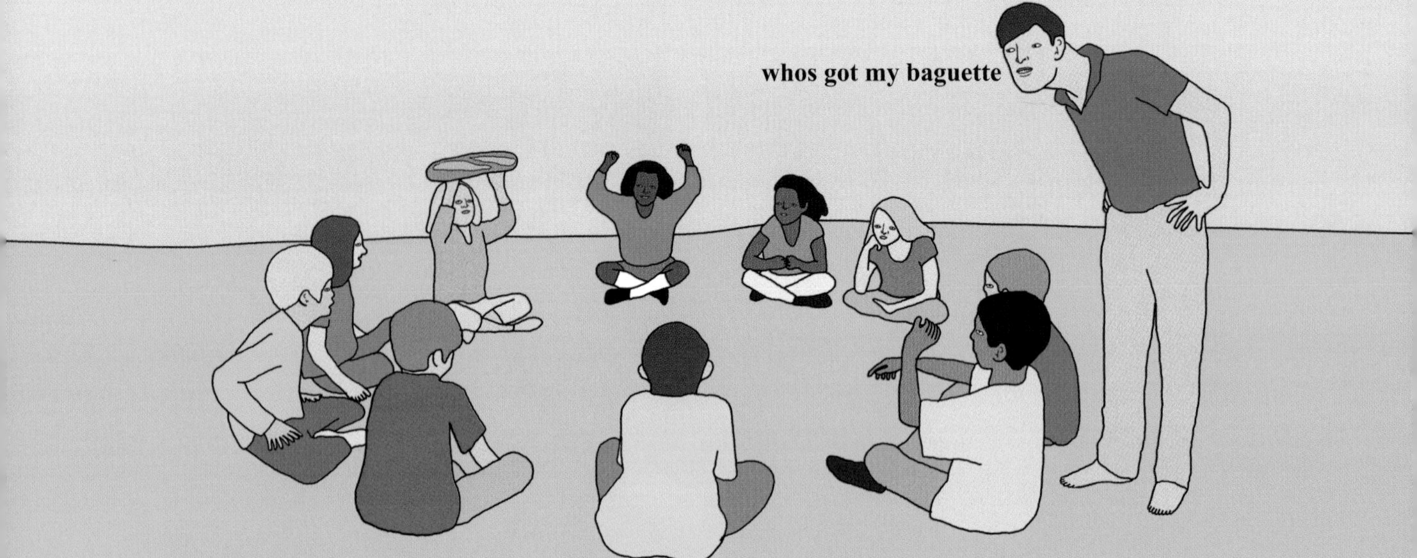
whos got my baguette

fascinating children

meet shirley he is 10 years old and he can taste what glass is thinking
just by looking out of windows and all of the other children at his school
call him a freak and they spit on top of his hair when he is on the bus and
they call him shy shirley but they dont know that he can taste what the
windows of the bus are thinking and as the children call him names
he always does a quiet laugh in the privacy of his own mouth
because he knows yes that is right shirley always knows

the school bus

when the winter comes papa will take his top off
and lie down on the front side of his body
and let his children bathe in the warming
heat of his back to help them survive
the deathly cold

thank you papa
for your warmth

it is fine

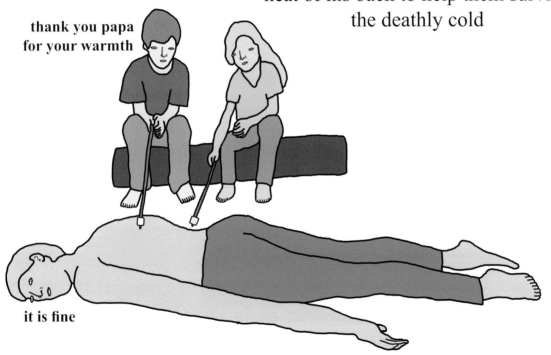

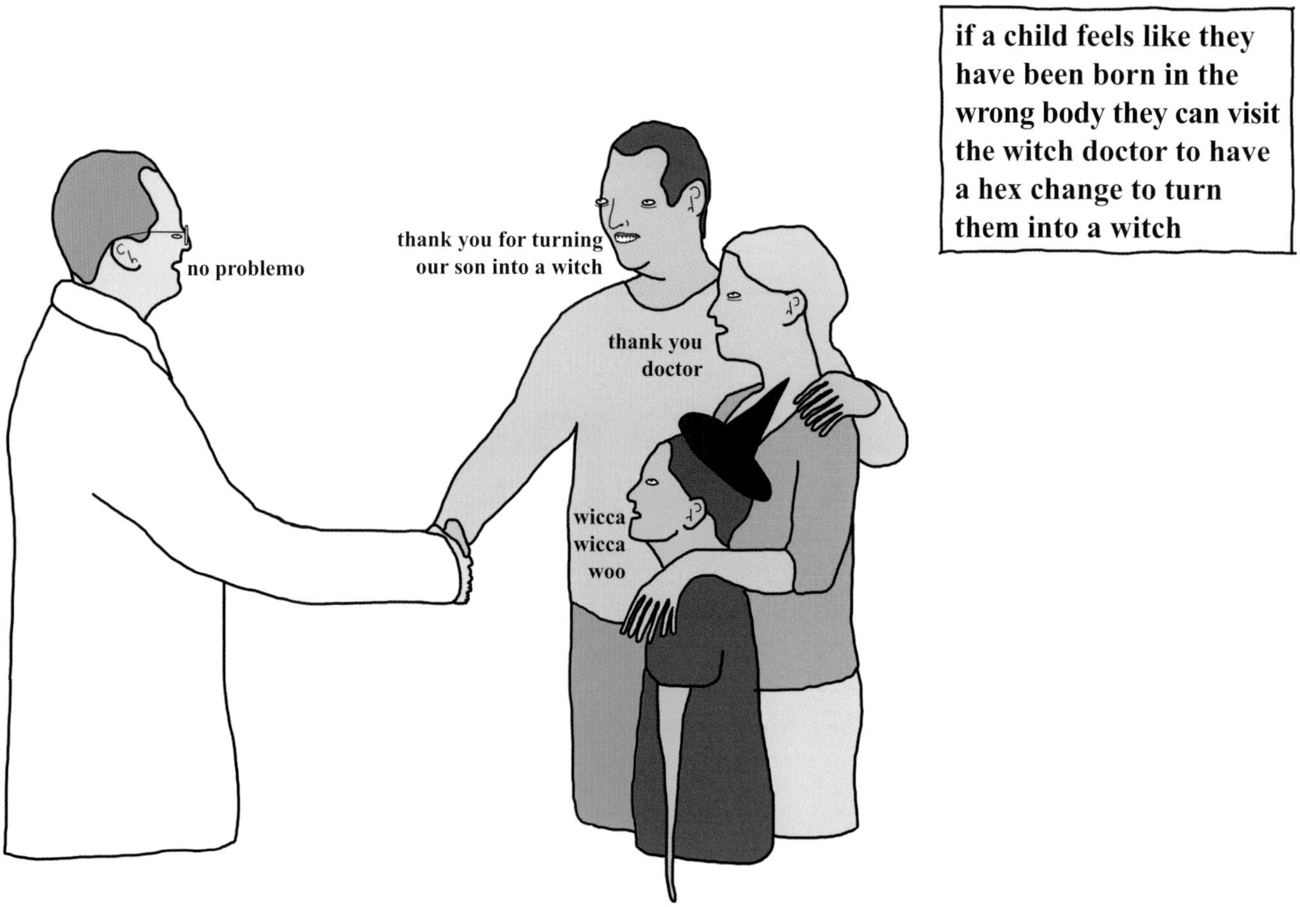
if a child feels like they have been born in the wrong body they can visit the witch doctor to have a hex change to turn them into a witch
no problemo
thank you for turning our son into a witch
thank you doctor
wicca wicca woo

teens

inside of a teens brain

dolphins
alone
loom bands
body hare
bread
feelings
what is the point
fear of the night
why am i so cold
the cloth witch

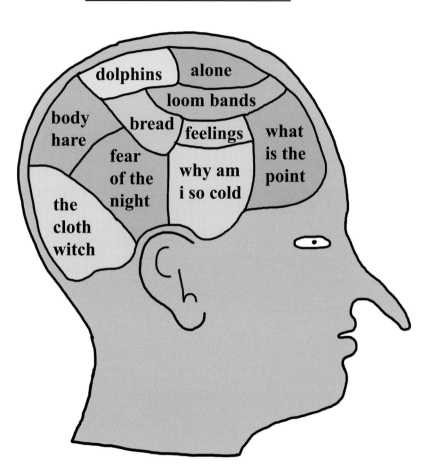

as soon as a person becomes a teenager they will notice that their body is changing a lot the first change that they will notice is that their neck will swell to the size of a mans head scientists call this the swollen necklace

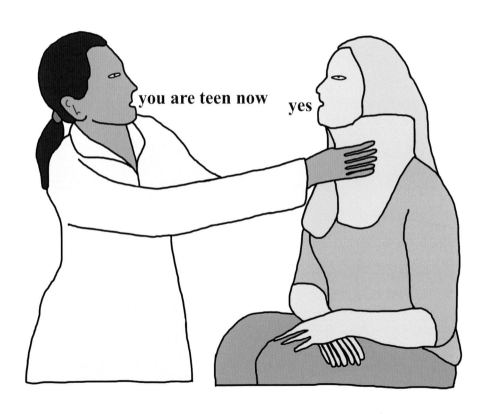

after the swollen necklace a teen will start to get spots on their face

other names for spots are:
pomples
egg heads
zeets
pussy lumps
crow droppings
face keepers
jills
cream puffs
plif dumplings

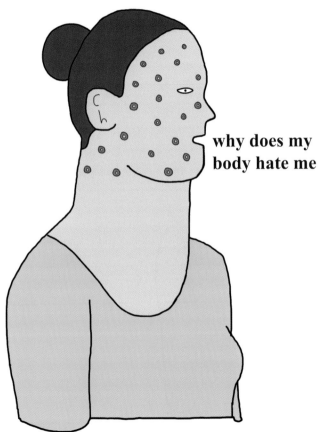

**why does my
body hate me**

body hare

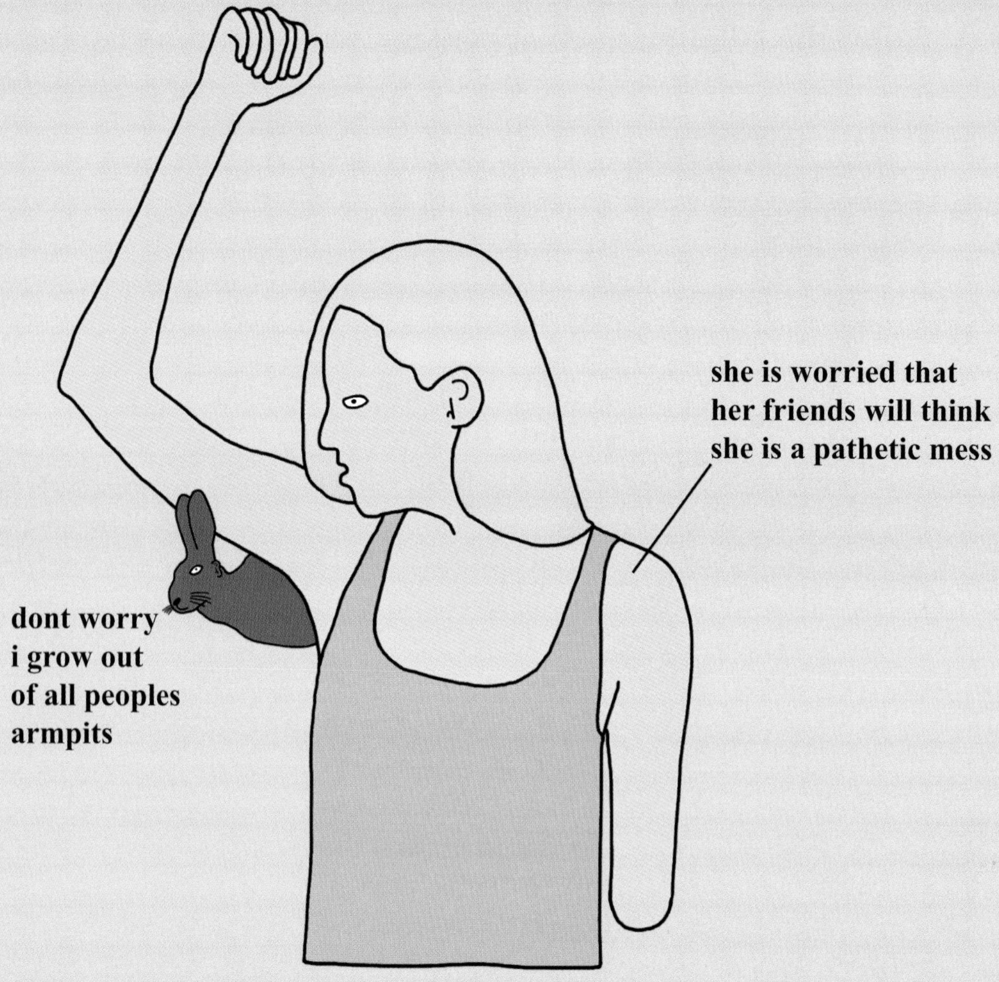

she is worried that
her friends will think
she is a pathetic mess
dont worry
i grow out
of all peoples
armpits

the body hare is a creature that starts to grow out of
your armpits when you are about 13 or 14 years old
at first it can be quite strange to get used to because
it has never been there before but after a little while
you will get used to it and soon enough you will
be combing it and showing it off to all of your
friends at the local rituals

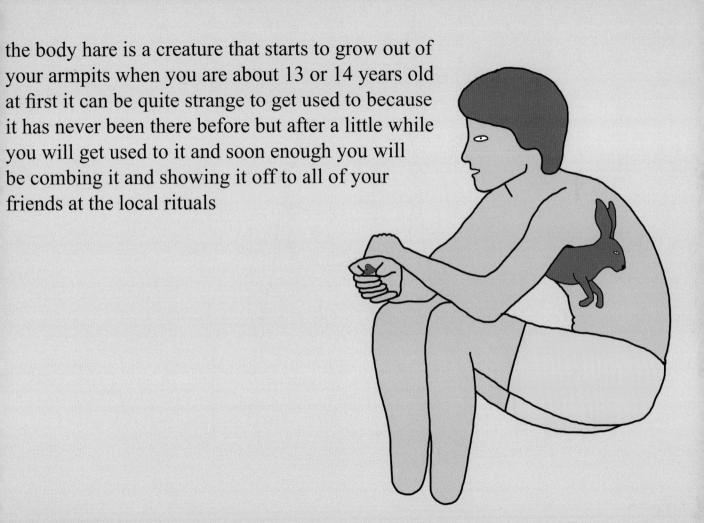

teens learn how to shave at 15 years old

no more face
lice for me

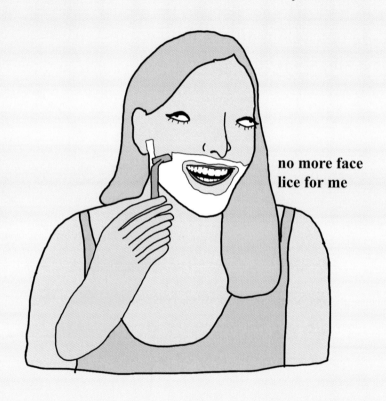

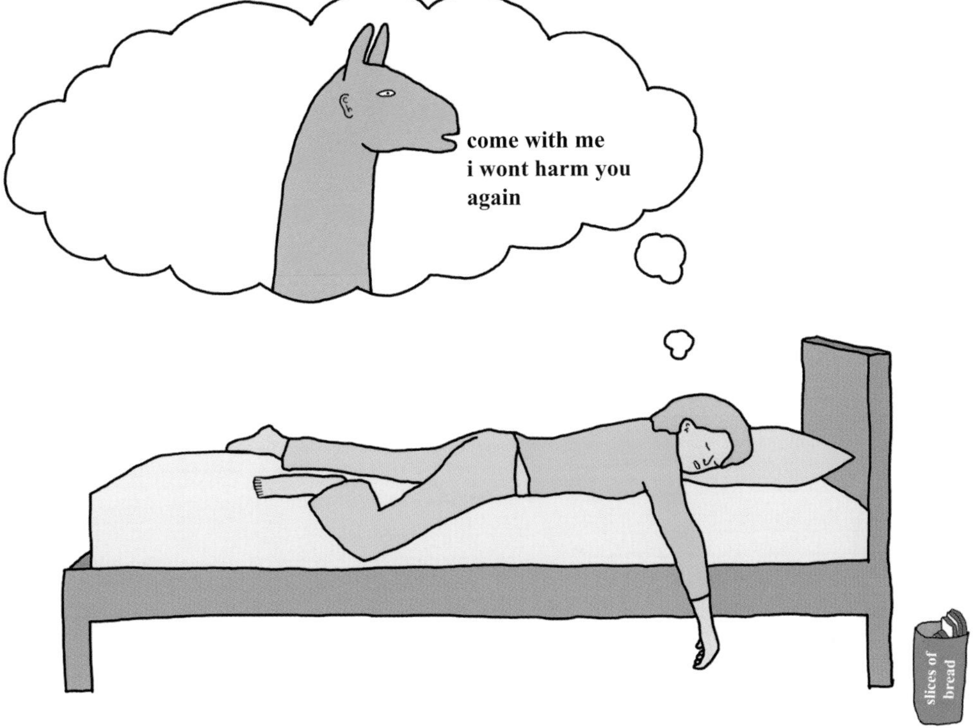
come with me
i wont harm you
again
slices of bread

teens need to sleep for 369 hours a week
or their bodies will shrivel up and die

a teenagers main way of having a chat
with other teens is by doing a texting

texting is like talking but instead of using
your throat to tell someones ears how you feel
you use your finger to speak your feelings onto
your telephone and into the other persons eyes

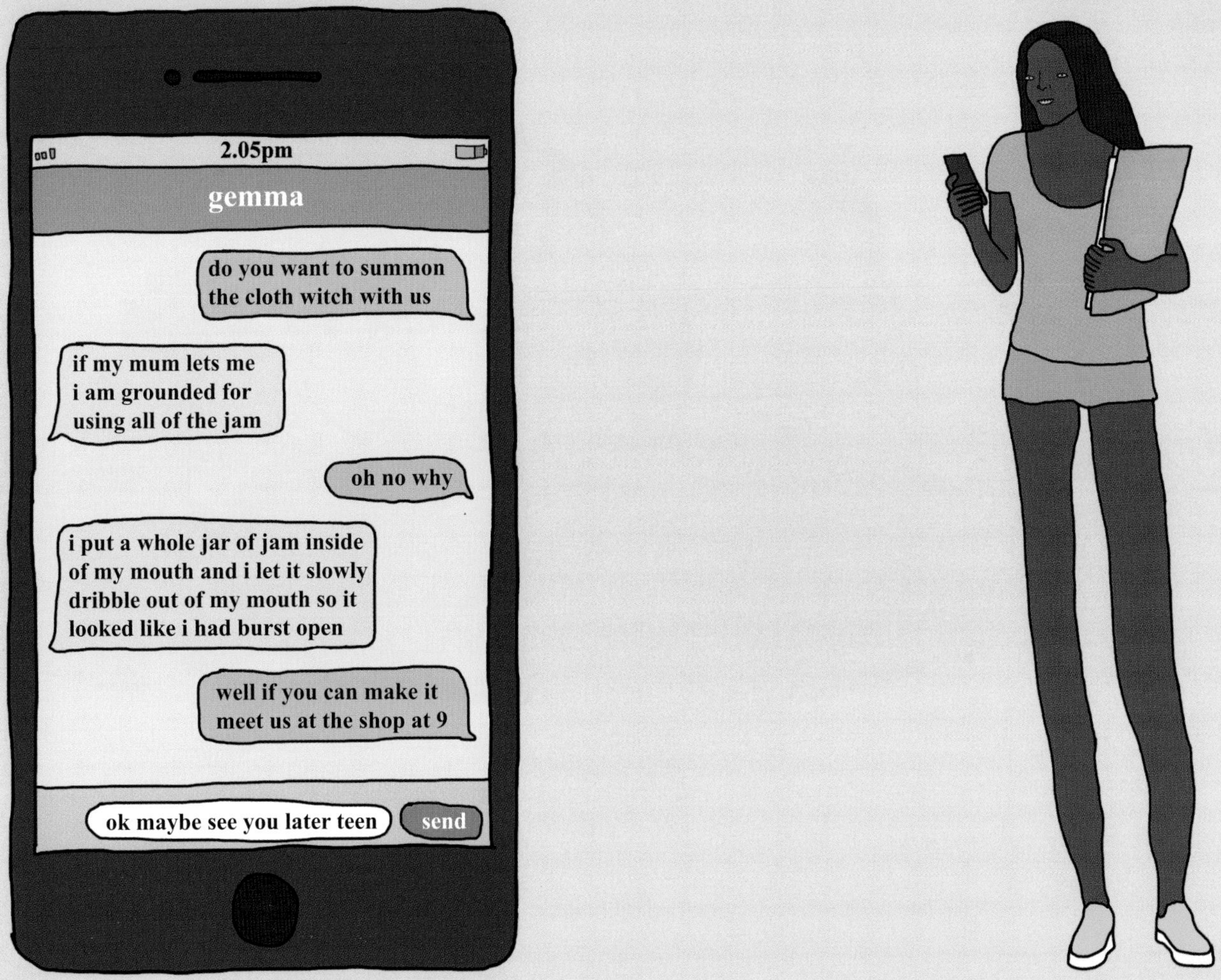
2.05pm
gemma
do you want to summon the cloth witch with us
if my mum lets me i am grounded for using all of the jam
oh no why
i put a whole jar of jam inside of my mouth and i let it slowly dribble out of my mouth so it looked like i had burst open
well if you can make it meet us at the shop at 9
ok maybe see you later teen
send

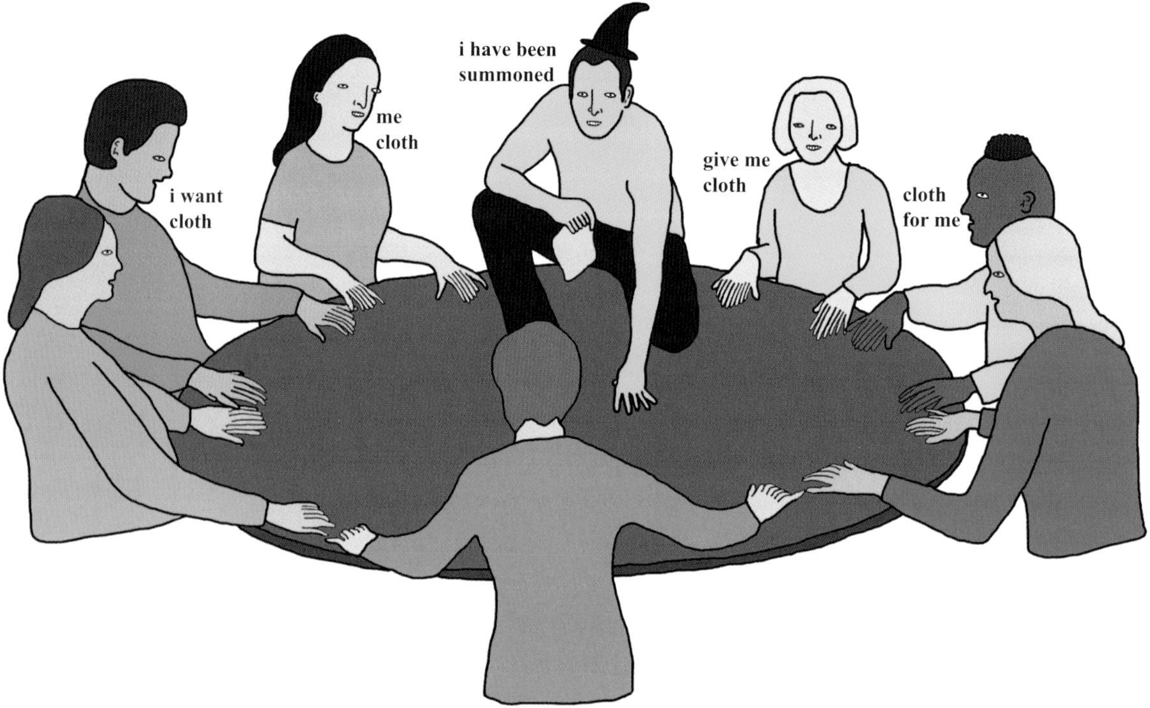
i want
cloth
me
cloth
i have been
summoned
give me
cloth
cloth
for me

a fun thing for teens to do together is a ritual

on thursday nights the local teens of the village get together to summon the cloth witch in the hope that he will bring them some cloth

the teen who has been given the most cloth at the end of the year will be chosen by the cloth witch to leave with him into the night

some people say that the cloth witch keeps the teens for his slave and forces them to make cloth in his castle

other people say that he takes care of them and he makes them beautiful cloth outfits for them to have a wear of but who knows because that is the mystery of the cloth witch

nice style
thanks teen friend

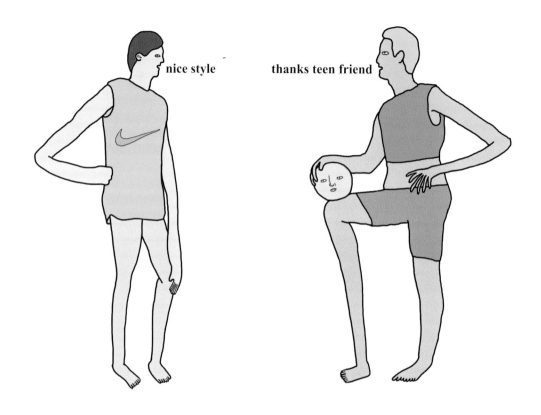

looking stylish is an important part of being a teen
if you dont look stylish then you look like an idiot
and if you look like an idiot then you wont get any texts

teen life

the worlds first style magazine for depressed teens

win
a beautiful
lace glove that
has got long
plastic beige
fingers

do you have a bread
helmet yet

learn how to
make your
very own
bread helmet
on page 12

make it
wear it
swallow it

also inside
today:

exclusive
interview
with the
cloth witch

and

meet the teen
who can
sniff the
sound
of her
own
name

bread helmets
the next teen craze

kissing is a romantic way for people to show that they like each other most people will have their first kiss at 16 years old and if you would like to try a kiss but are feeling a bit nervous about how to do one then here is some of the most popular kisses to help you decide which one to do

the spit in my mouth - spitting in the person you loves mouth is the most romantic thing that you can do with a mouth and all that you need to be able to do it is a couple of mouths and some spit

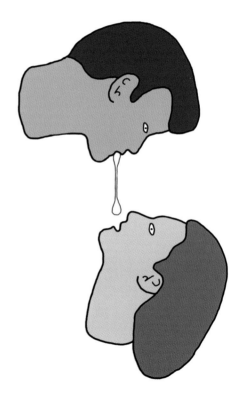

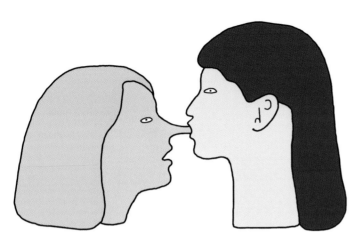

the suck - put the nose of your sweet girl inside of your mouth and do a thick suck so that their nose goes all of the way down your throat

the dolphin - make your tongue into the shape of a dolphin and dip its face in and out of your lovers mouth like a dolphin dipping its face in and out of a meat cave

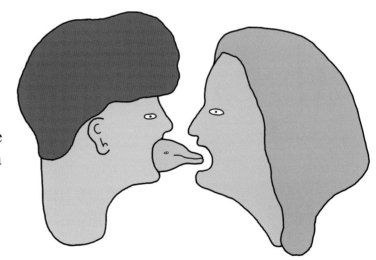

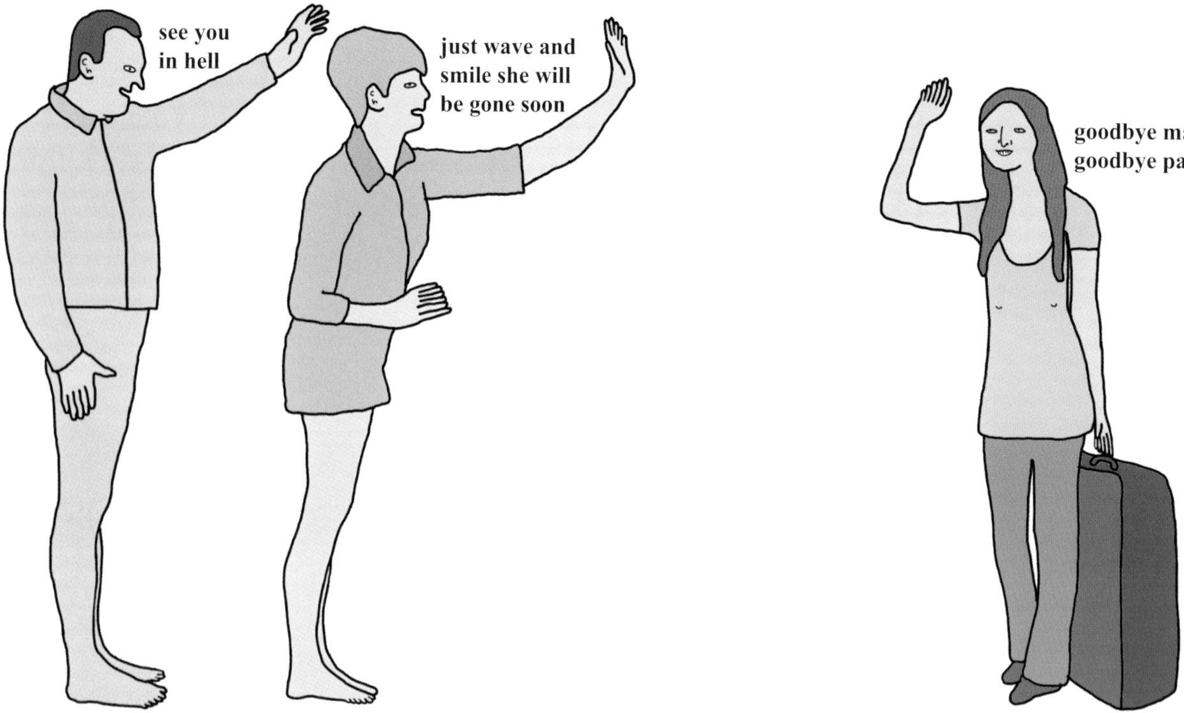

see you
in hell
just wave and
smile she will
be gone soon
goodbye mama
goodbye papa

now it is time for you to leave home
and to make a life of your very own
but wherever you finish or whatever you start
always keep a slice of home tucked inside of your heart

starting a new life away from home can be hard at first
but the friendship prince is here to guide you

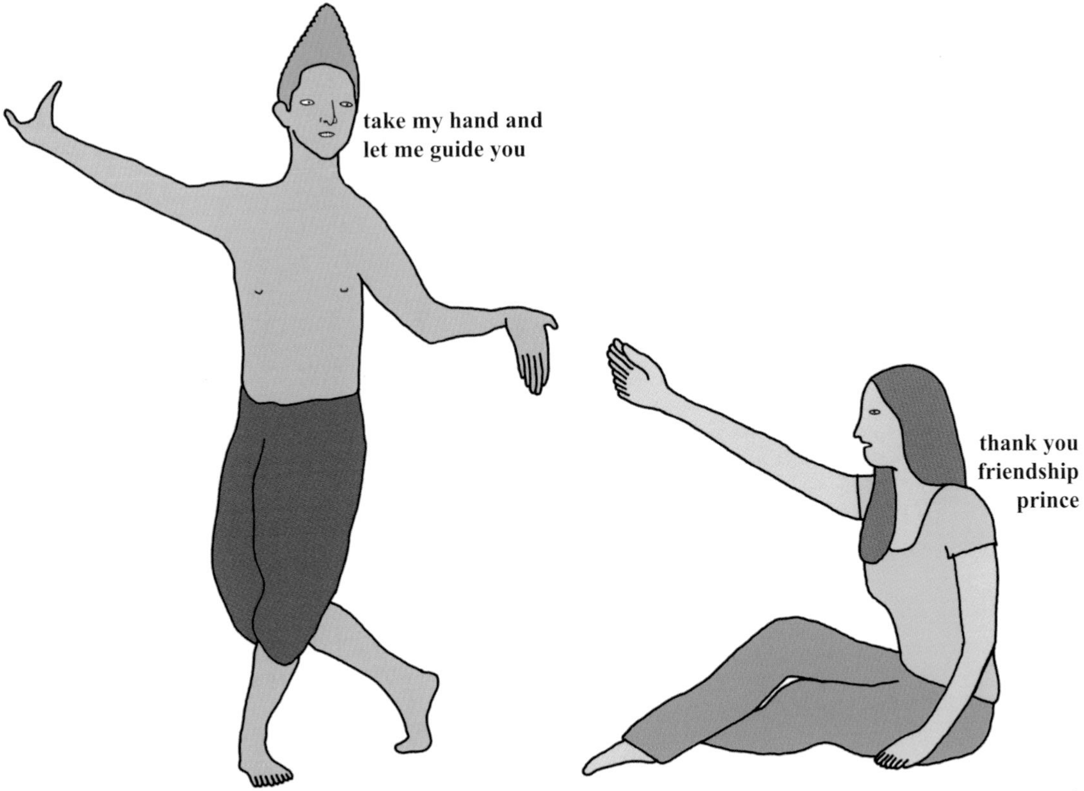
take my hand and let me guide you
thank you friendship prince

adult

congratulations for getting this far
you are a adult now well done

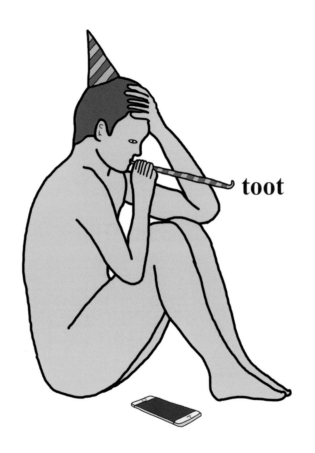

toot

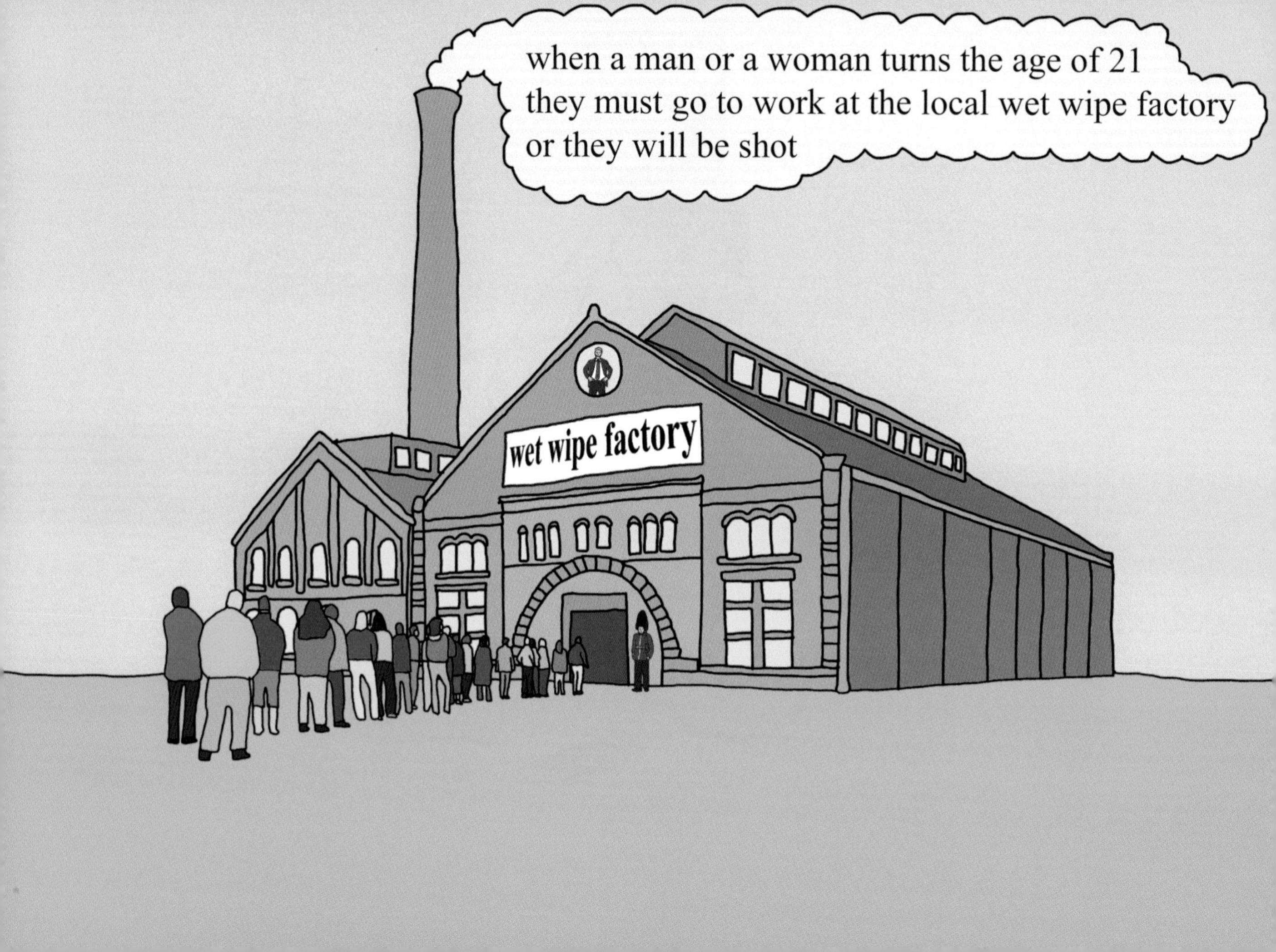
when a man or a woman turns the age of 21
they must go to work at the local wet wipe factory
or they will be shot
wet wipe factory

fact of life

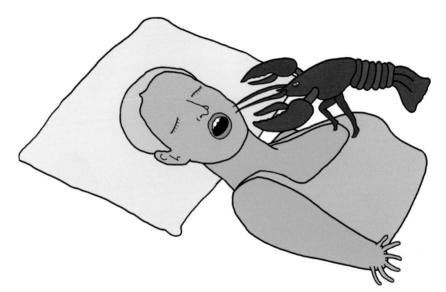

the average person swallows 8 lobsters in their sleep every year

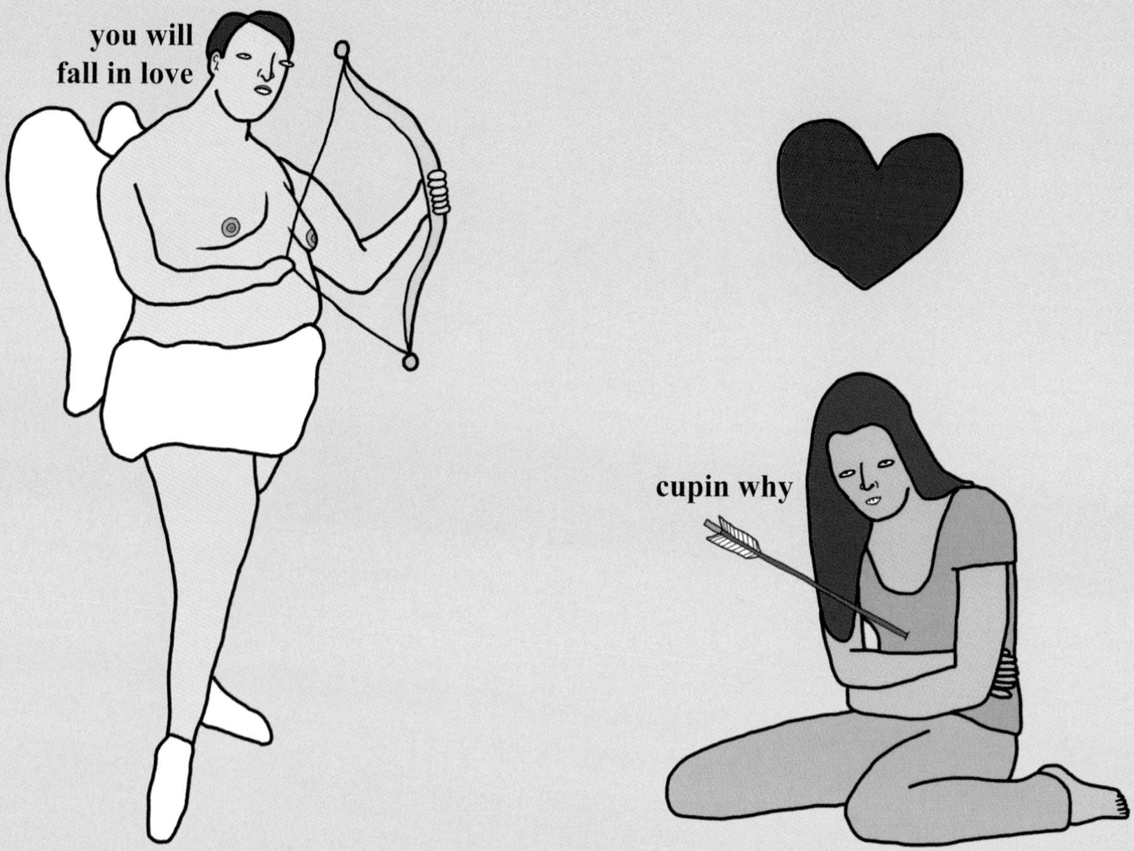
you will
fall in love
cupin why

falling in love can be hard

finding the right person to fall in love with can be even harder

that is why cupin is here to help us

cupin is the god of love and he will shoot you with his poisonous arrow
that has been dipped in his spit to make people fall in love with you

so you wont be alone forever

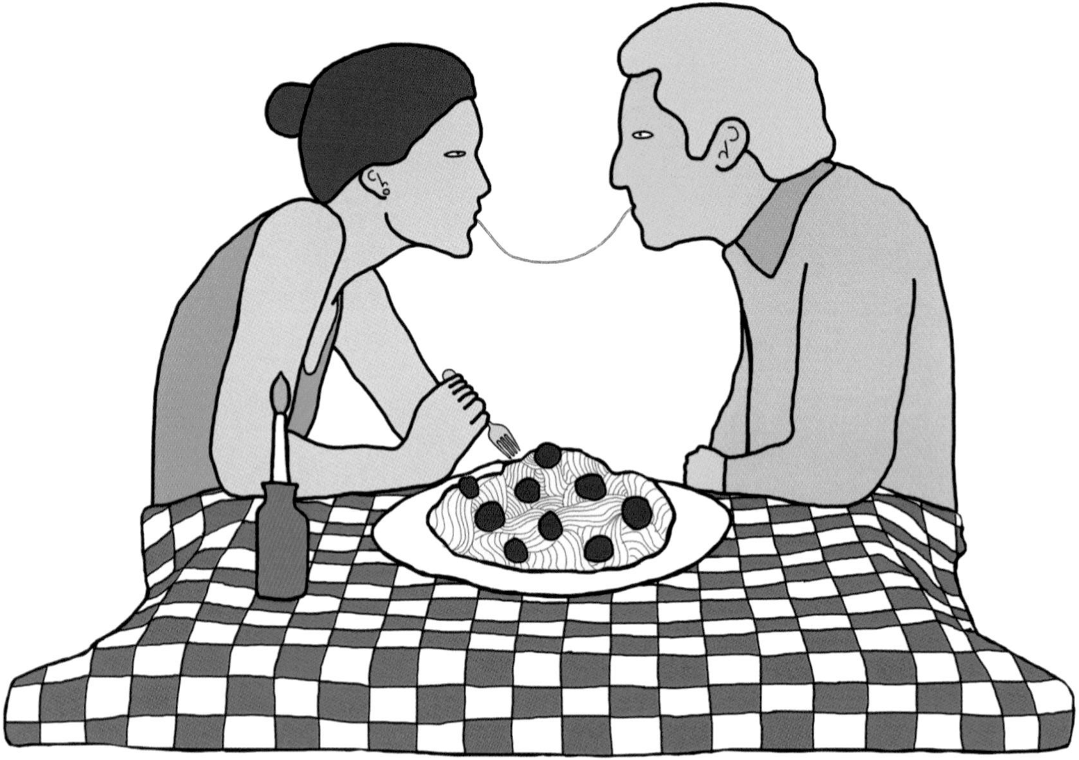

dating is a fun way of trying to find someone like you who doesnt want to die alone

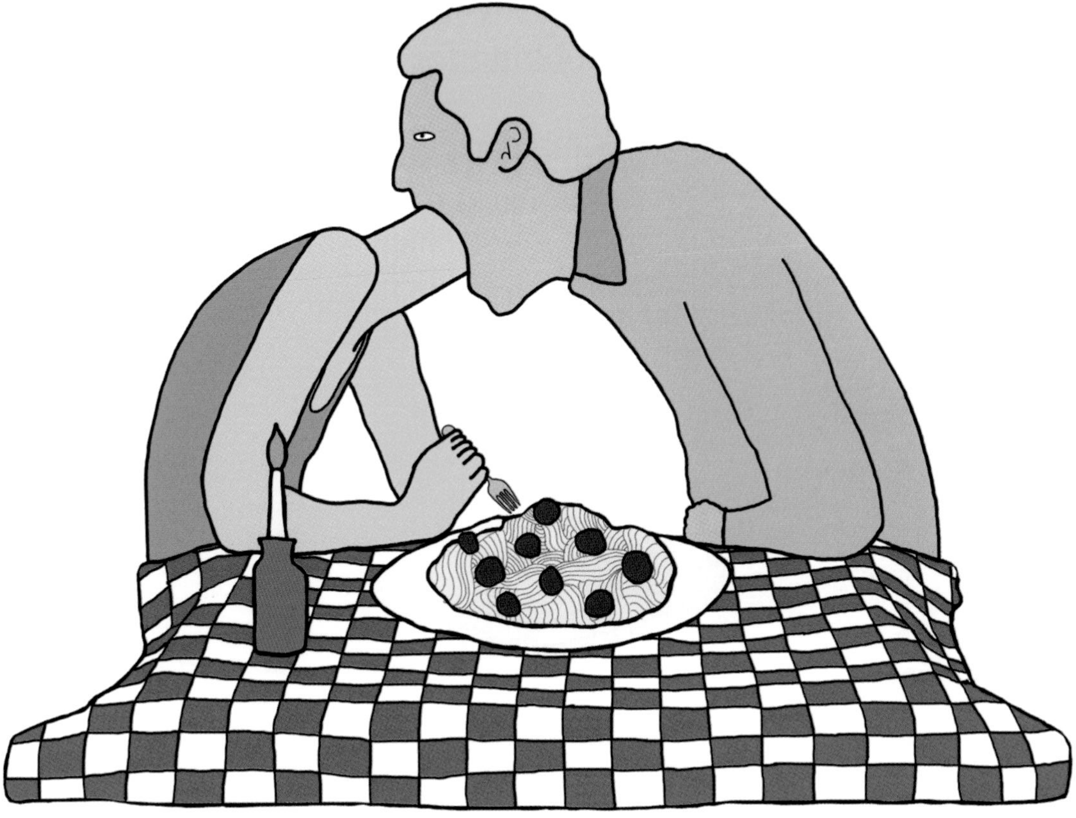

a good place to go for a date is to a restaurant

online dating is a good way to meet other lonely people
who are looking for a extra slice of spice in their life

this is liz she is 33 years old and she spends
the lonely nights looking for someone who
will fall in love with her

hi looking for spice

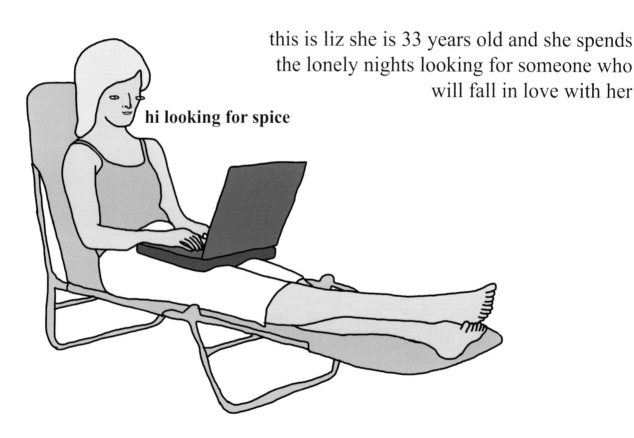

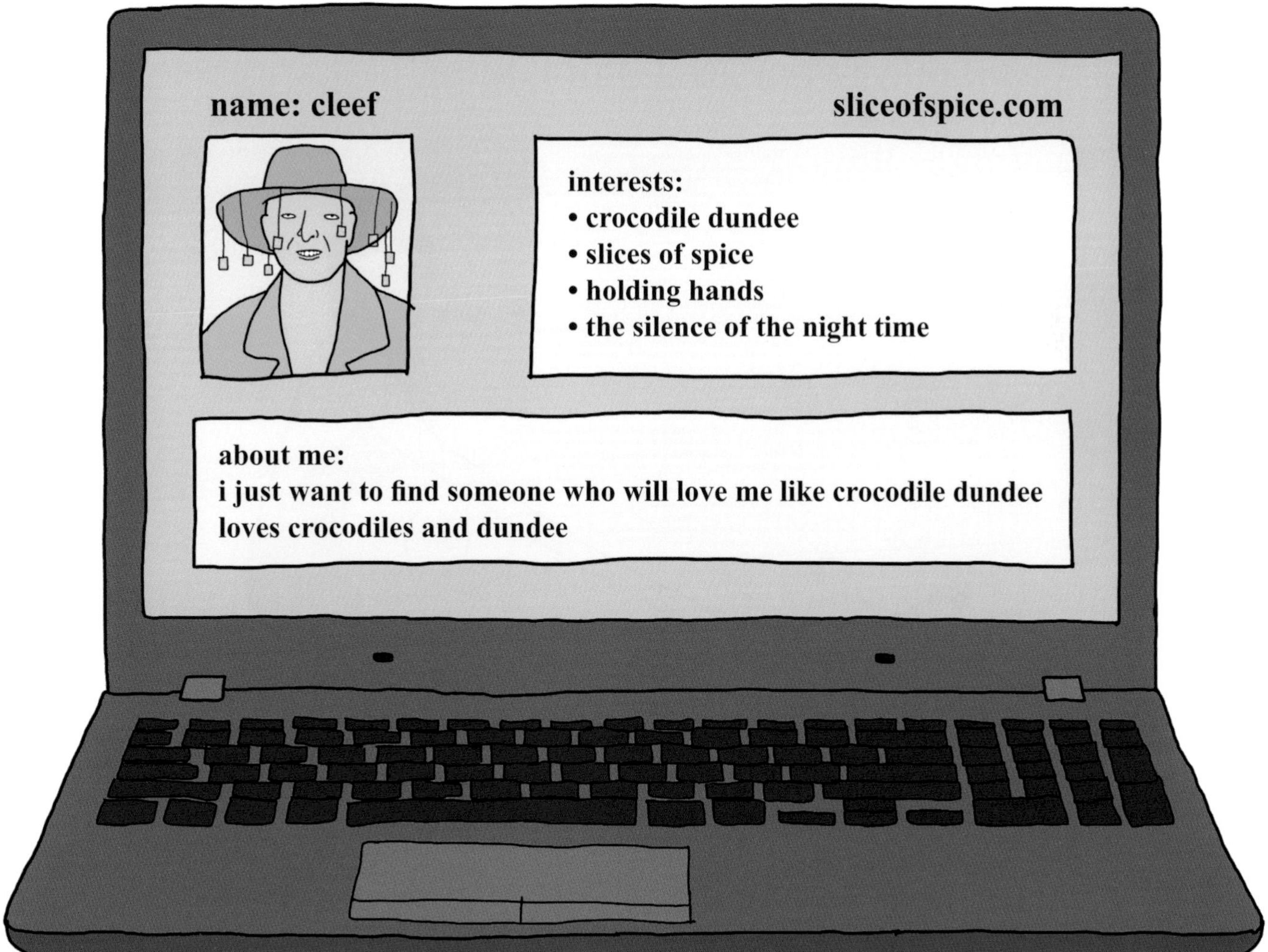
name: cleef
sliceofspice.com
interests:
• crocodile dundee
• slices of spice
• holding hands
• the silence of the night time
about me:
i just want to find someone who will love me like crocodile dundee loves crocodiles and dundee

just before a lady gets married she will have a hen party

wish me luck

the bride to be will milk a hen of her choice

good luck

and then she will drink the milk with her friends
to bring her good luck for when she is married

the night before a man gets married he will have a stag party

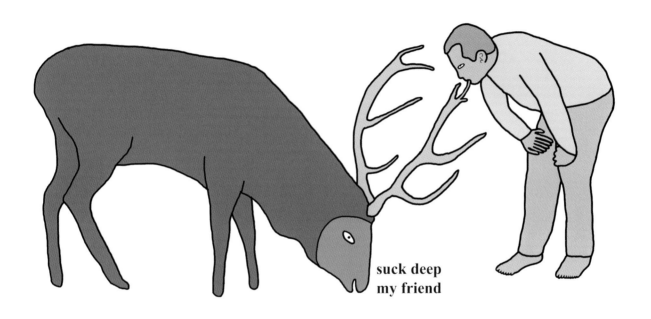

suck deep
my friend

the male bride to be will be taken to a field by his friend and he will
suck a stags antlers for up to 8 hours to help drive bad spirits away

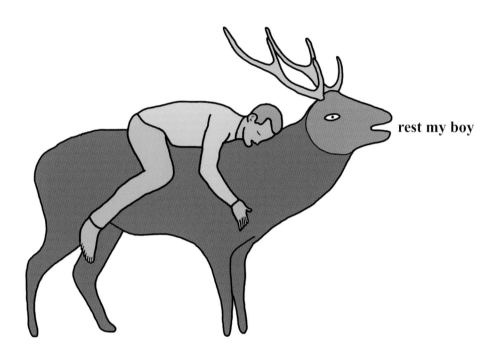

rest my boy

the man will then be carried to his wedding by the stag
while he enjoys a restful sleep upon its warming brown back

marriage

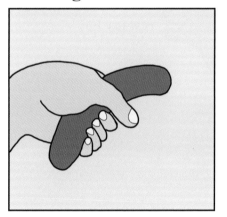 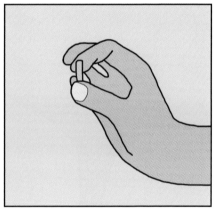 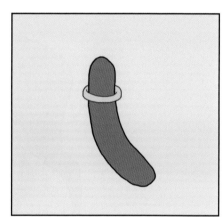

i have found
the love of my life
and my closest
friend

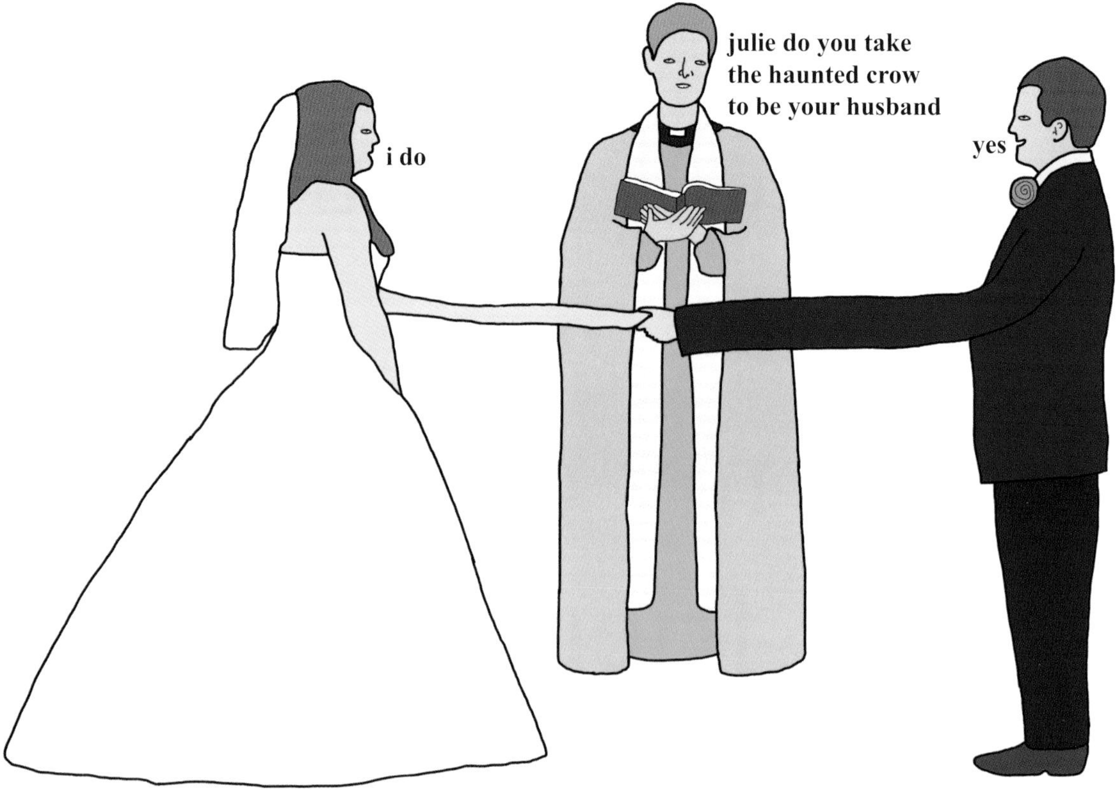
julie do you take
the haunted crow
to be your husband
i do
yes

the day has finally come for you to marry the man or woman of your dreams

once you are married
a hole will be cut out of the
bottom of the wedding cake

told you so

the groom will then wear the cake
on his head for the next year and a half
to prove to people that he now has a wife
and it wasnt all a lie

is this it

it is it

it is time for you to buy your first house
it is only small but a small house holds the
same amount of happiness as a big one so you will be fine

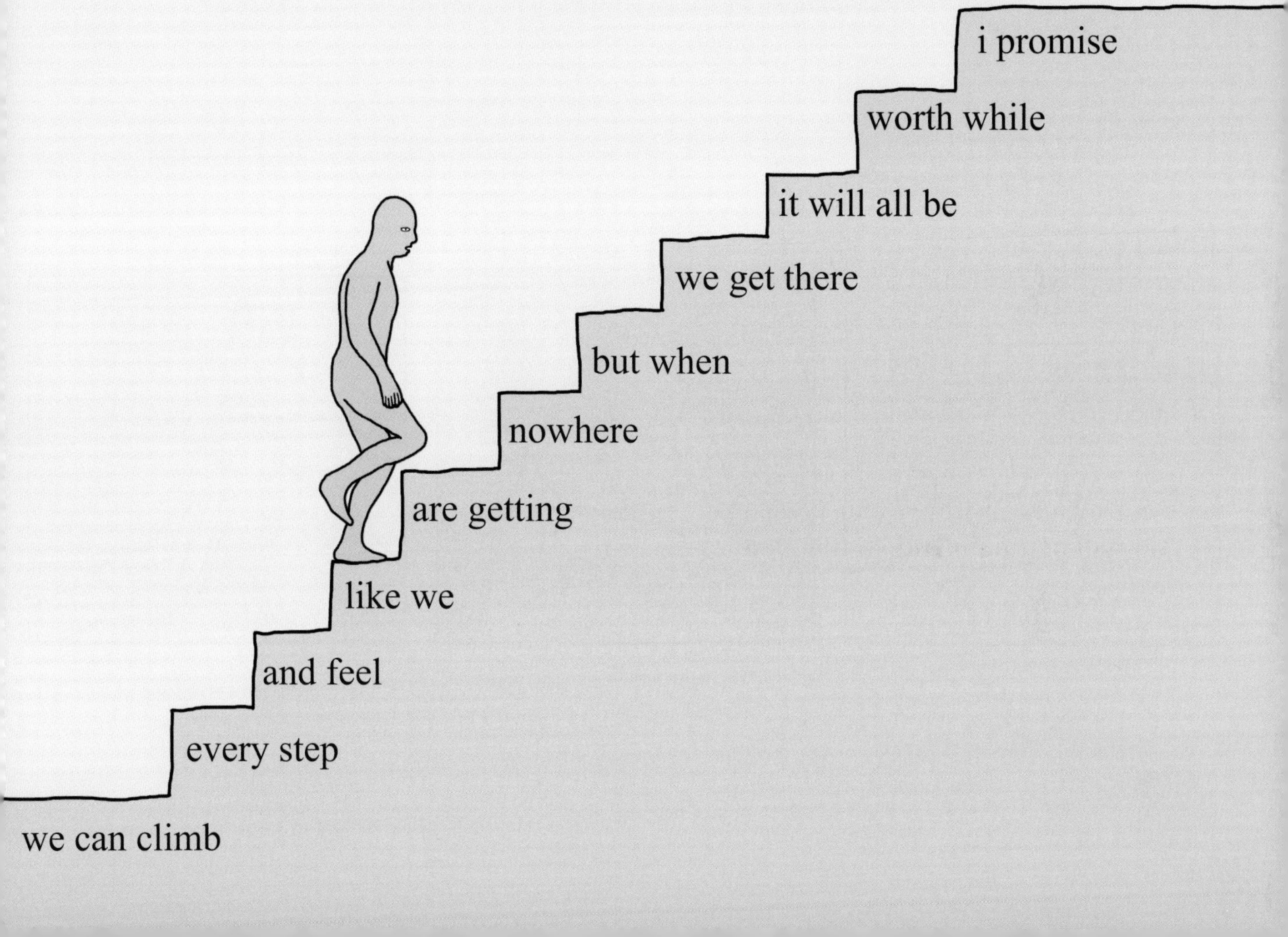
we can climb
every step
and feel
like we
are getting
nowhere
but when
we get there
it will all be
worth while
i promise

pets

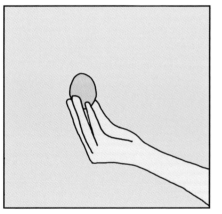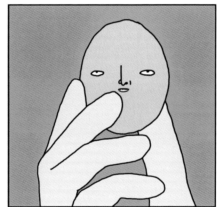

some people choose to keep a animal in their house this is called having a pet there is 4 different types of pets in the world and their names is called dogs cats little pinks and throat cauldrons but my best one is throat cauldrons because they are the most relaxing creatures in all of the world

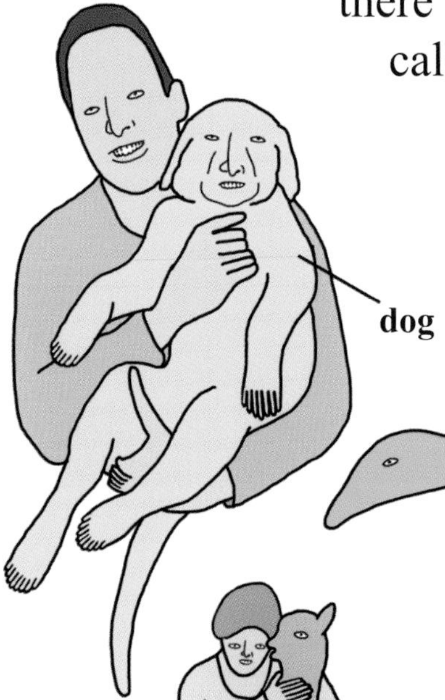
dog

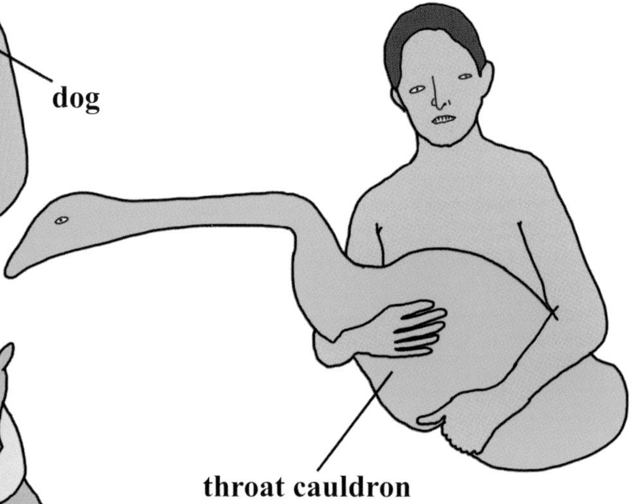
throat cauldron

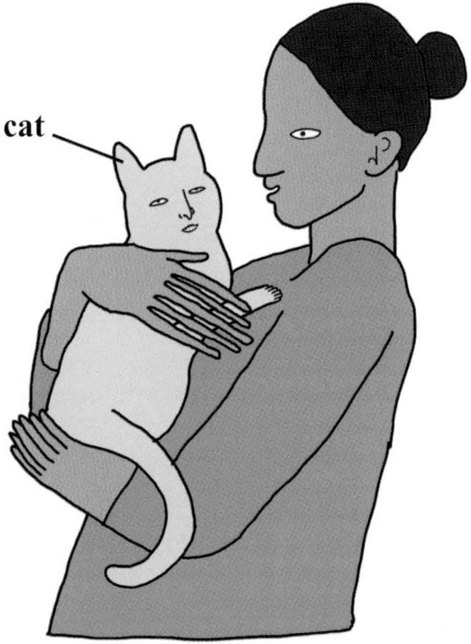
cat

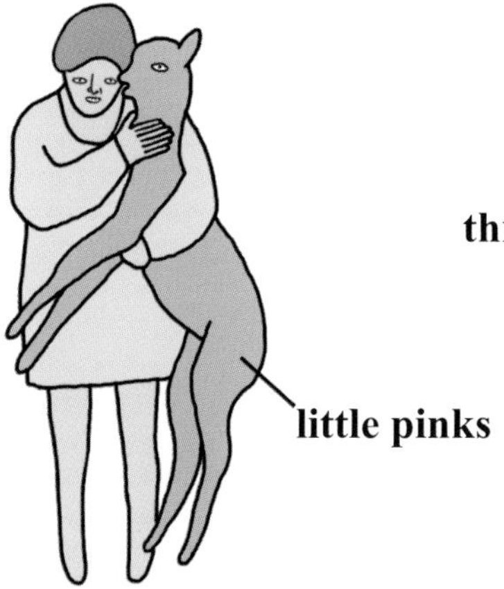
little pinks

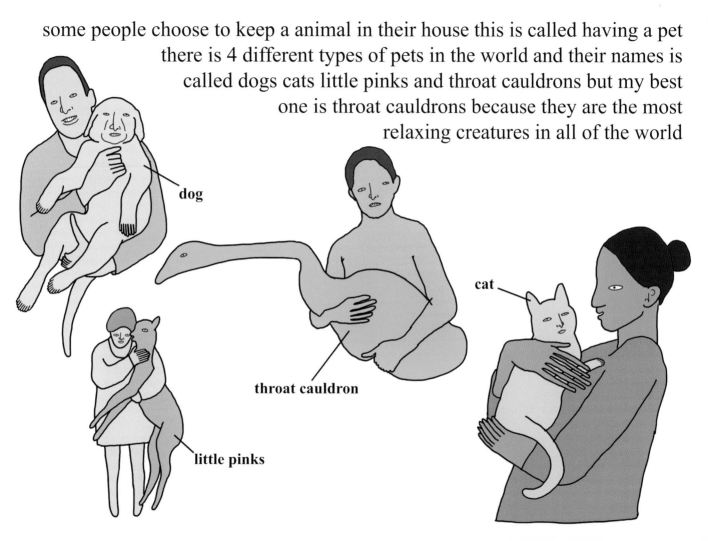

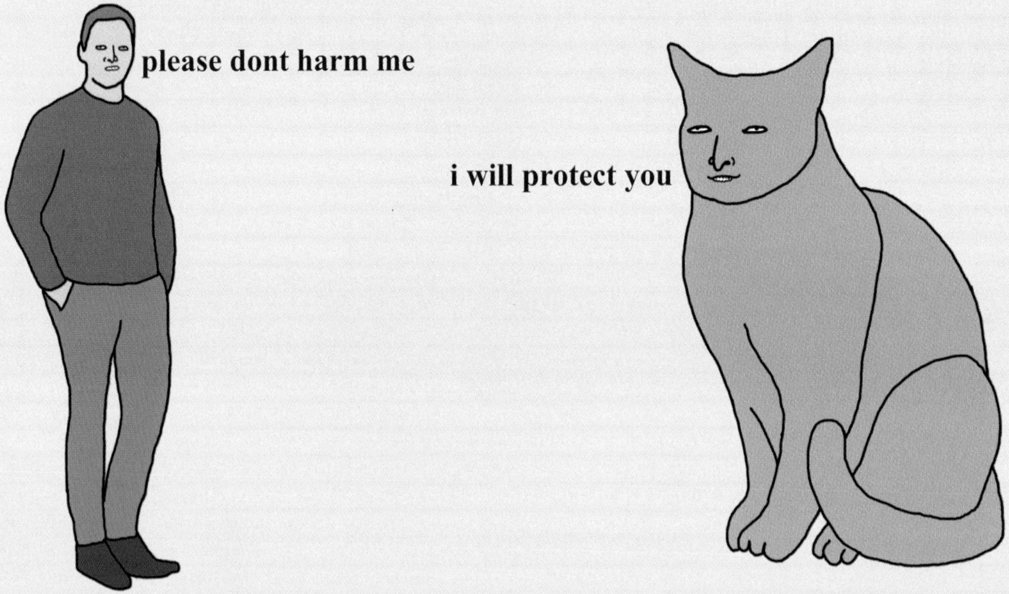
please dont harm me
i will protect you

at about the age of 32 some men will shrink to the size of a cat

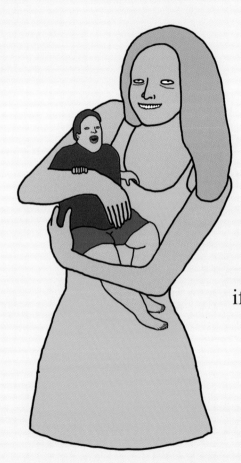

most men choose to stay this size and
live the rest of their life as small pets

health tip:
if there is a history of shrinking in your family
it is important to get yourself checked
at the doctors to make sure that you
wont shrink as well

now that you have found the person who you want to be with forever
you can start a family of your very own

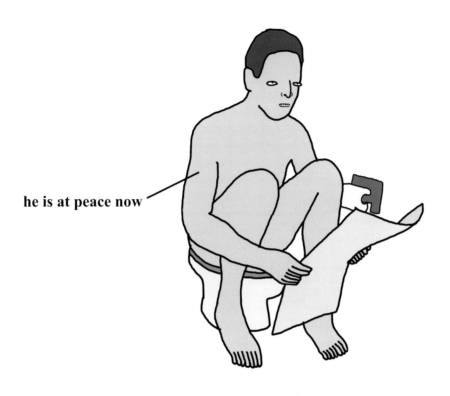

he is at peace now

papa will spend the next 15 years of his life on the toilet
to get some peace from his family

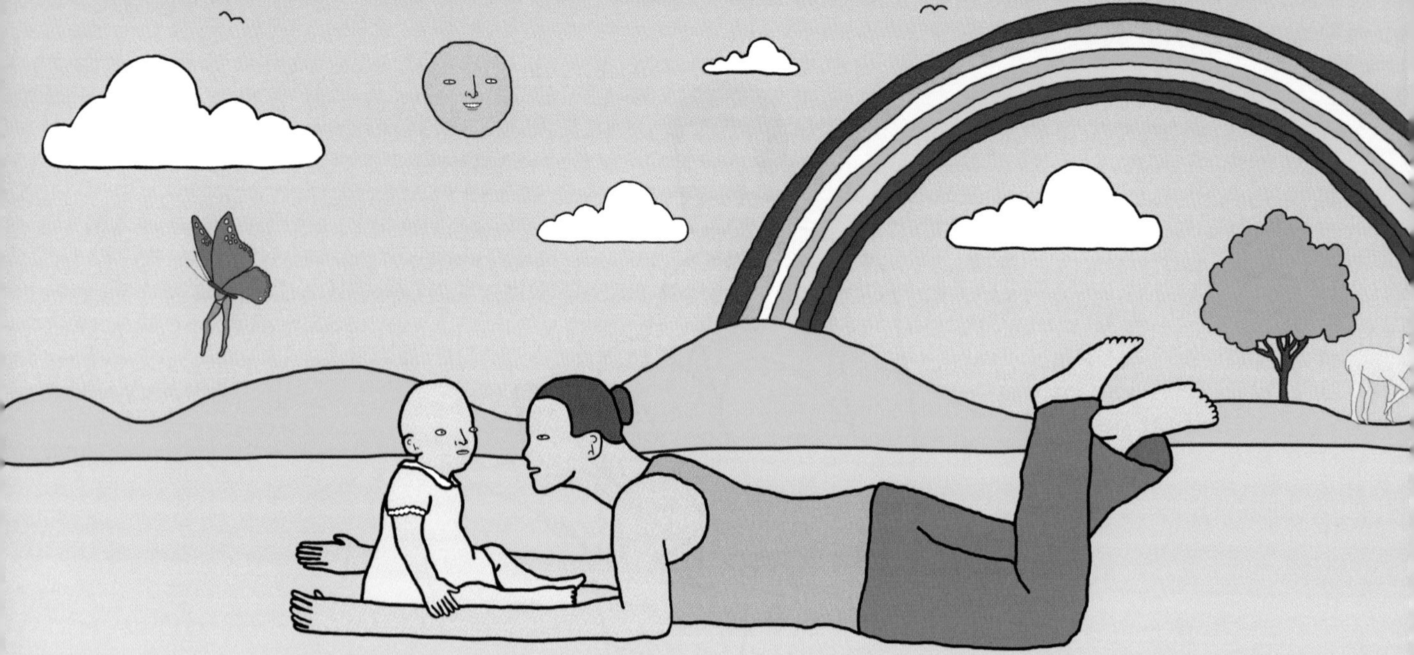

there is so much beauty in the world
but sometimes people dont see it
because they are too busy looking at their children

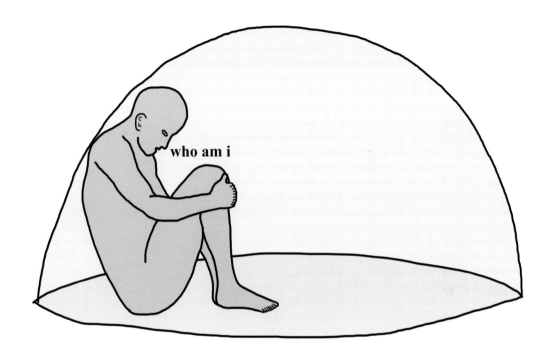

who am i

when people turn the age of 40 it is a tradition for them
to be given a large hollowed out see through dome to live inside
for up to one year to help them settle their thoughts about their life

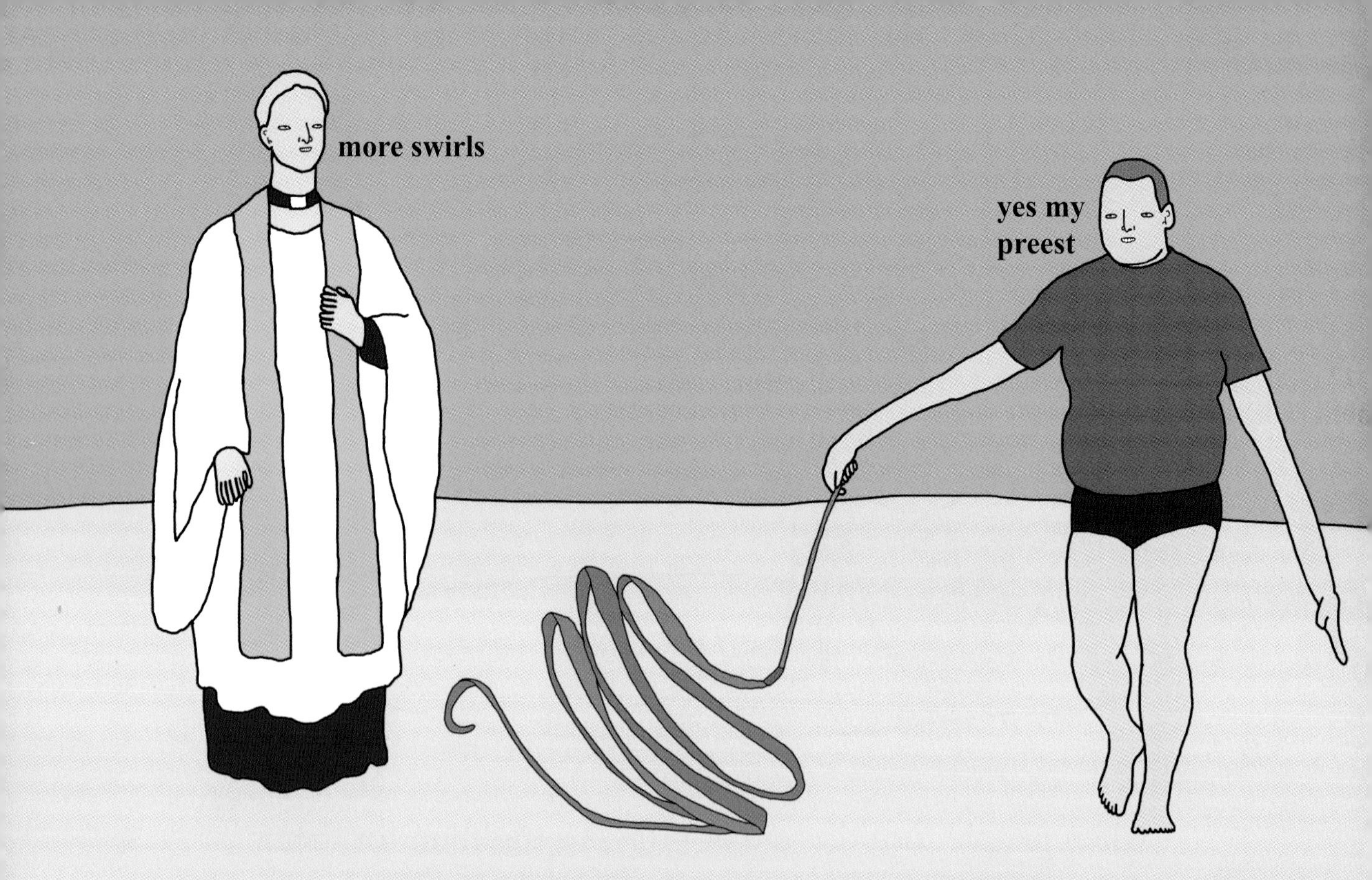
more swirls
yes my preest

on saturday nights the local dads get together
to perform gymnastics for the main priest of the village

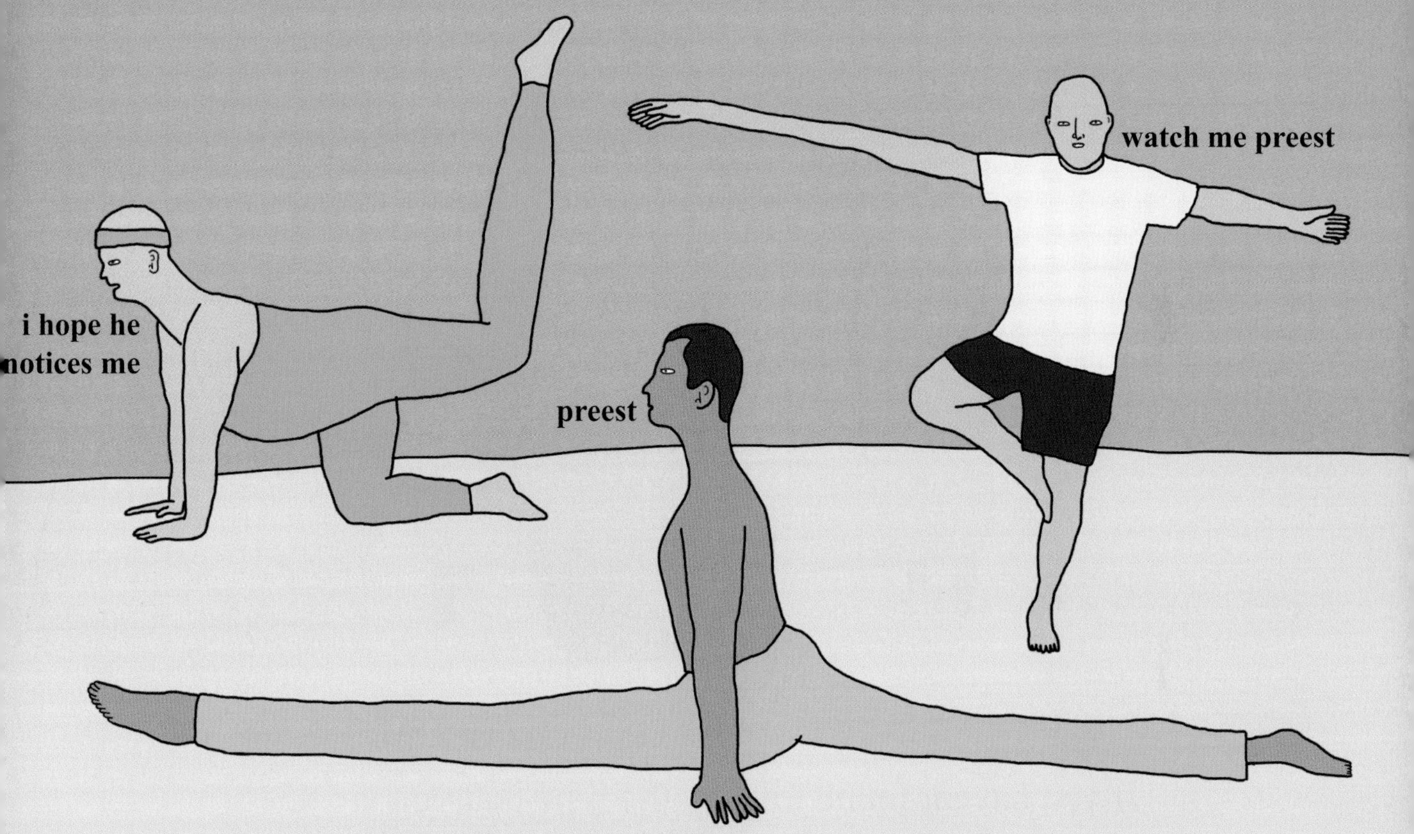

i hope he
notices me
preest
watch me preest

they will perform until the morning time
or until the priest closes his eyes

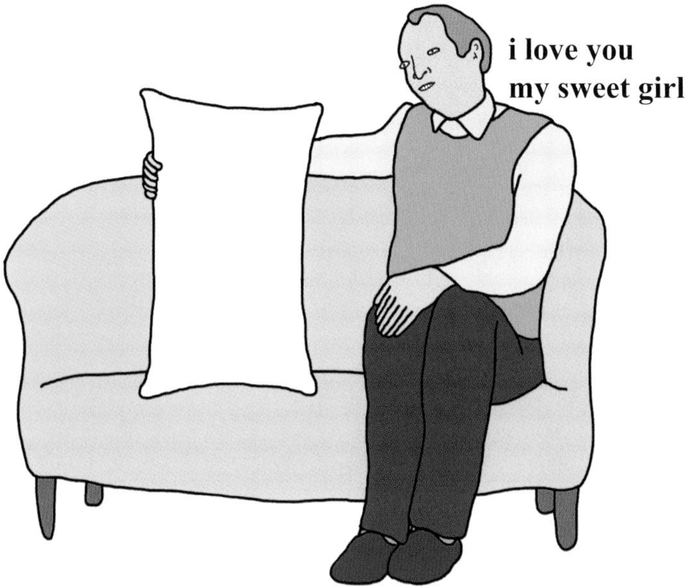
i love you
my sweet girl

if you havent found love by the time that you are 45
then you better get used to cuddling your pillow every night
until you are dead because she is your wife now

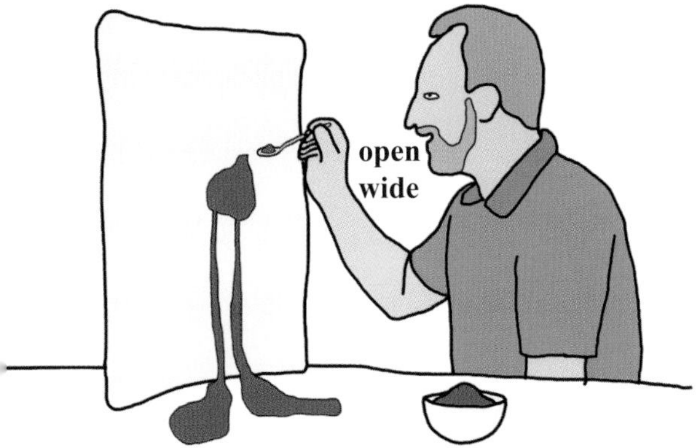
open
wide

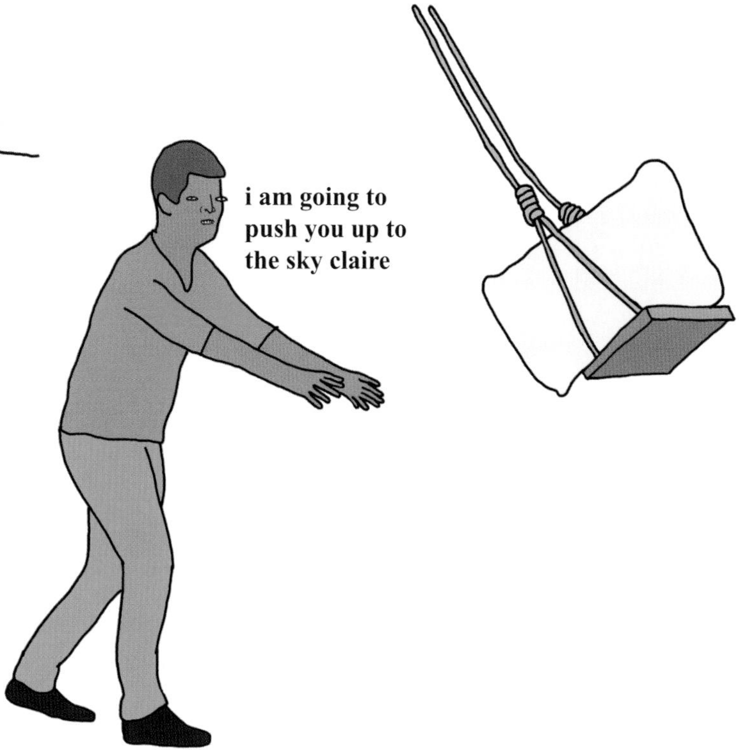
i am going to
push you up to
the sky claire

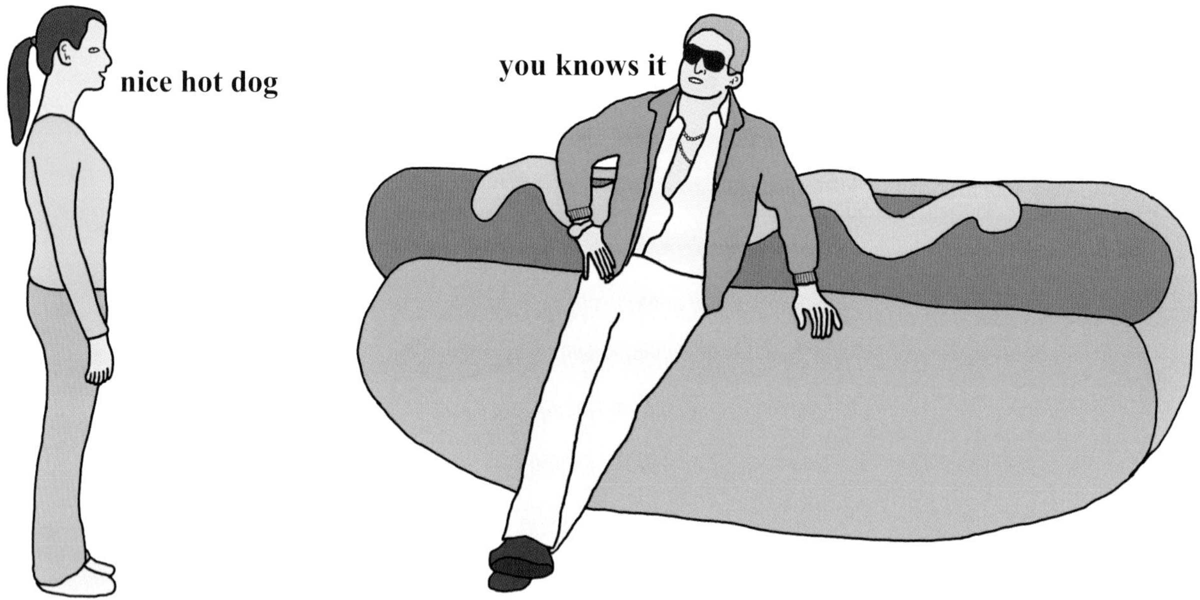
nice hot dog
you knows it

at the age of 50 some men will have a mid life crisis

a mid life crisis is when a person is frightened of becoming old and dying
so they spend all of their money on the biggest hot dog in town
to make people think that they are still young and fresh

this man is called craig but he has started to call himself the wasp
because he said that craig is such a old mans name and his wife
says that they could have used the money he spent on his hot dog
to go on a nice holiday together but he would rather spend all day
standing in the street outside of his house leaning on his hot dog
and winking at all of the ladies who walk past him but i think that
deep down he knows that his hot dog wont stay fresh forever and
death will soon find him

the feather witch

people may think that the most dangerous things in life is getting crushed by a horse or being poisoned by rat eggs but the main danger of human life is actually the feather witch and if you whisper feathers into a mirror three times then the feather witch will bring you a box of feathers to your house but be careful not to look into his eyes or you will be turned into a feather

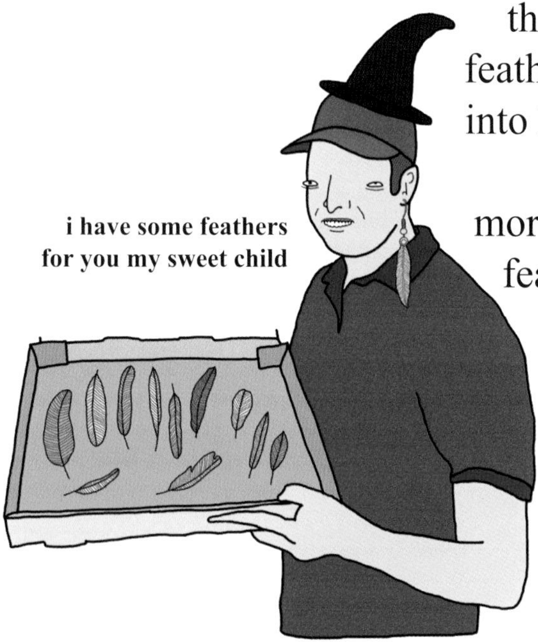
i have some feathers
for you my sweet child

more than 500 people every day are turned into feathers by the feather witch and that is why i think it is important for people to know not to look into his eyes when he comes to your house because even though feathers are beautiful they are not as beautiful as being alive the feather earring that the feather witch is having a wear of used to be the feather witches son and when the feather witch and his wifes son was born they was so happy but they was so scared at the same time because they knew that if their son ever looked into his fathers eyes then he would be no more so the feather witch always made sure to not look at his newborn son in his eyes but then one night their son was crying in the night time and the feather witches wife said it was his turn to get the baby back to sleep so the feather witch got out of his bed feeling halfway asleep and he went into his sons room and he turned on the light and then before he could even realise what he had done his son had already looked into his eyes and he was instantly turned into a feather so that is why the feather witch always has a wear of that feather on his ear so his son will always be close to him even though he had to go away so soon

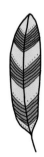

old age

inside of a old persons mind

death
bees
pain
alone
sleep
buttons

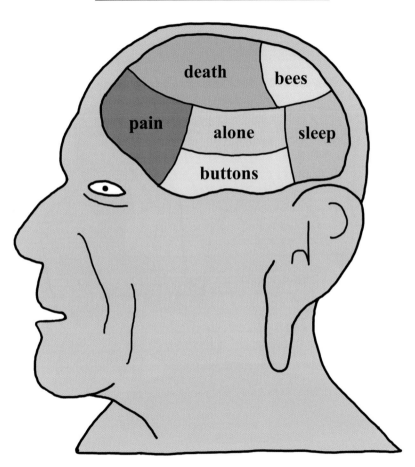

how to tell you have become old:

you start to smell of fireplaces

what is
it doctor
you smell of
fireplaces

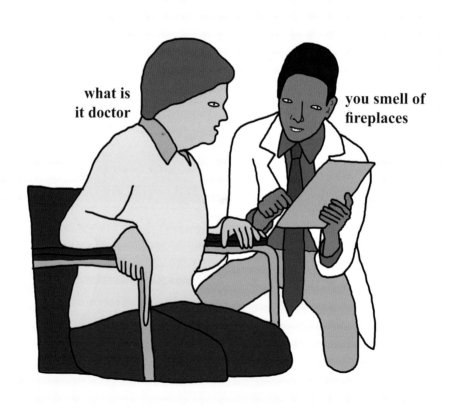

in a single lifetime the human eye sees more than 400 different things

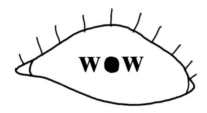

the power of the human eye

old peoples diets:

old people need to eat all of the right things
to try and keep them alive for a extra day so they can see
how much fun their families are having without them

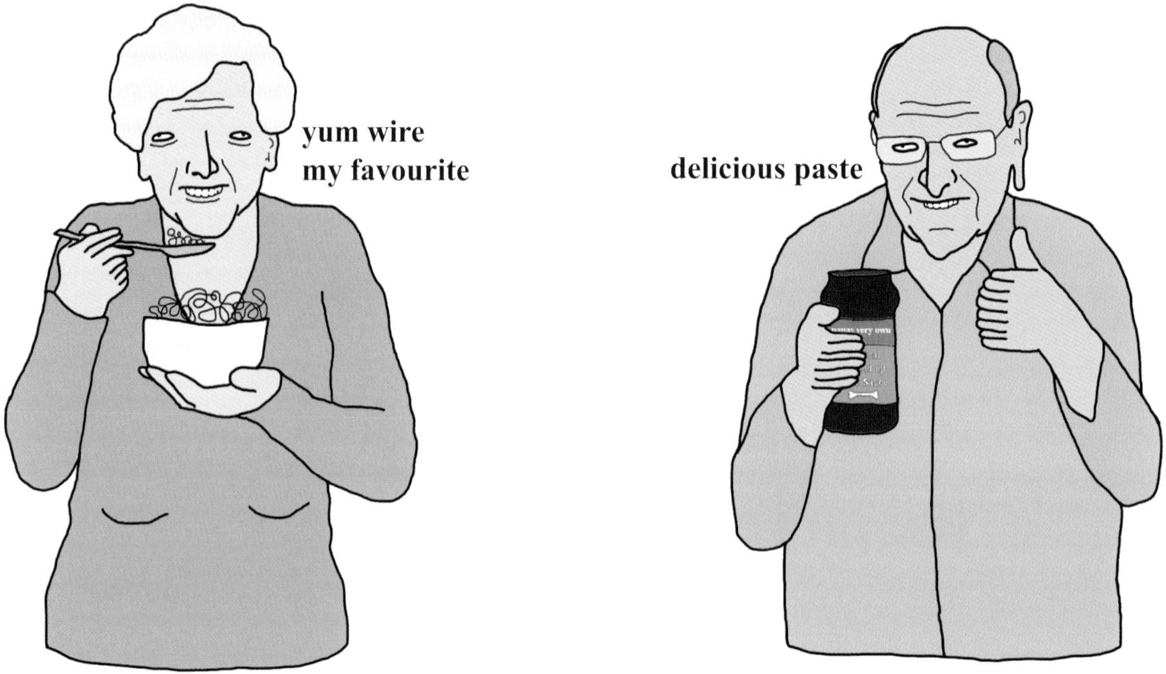
yum wire
my favourite
delicious paste

wire - what old people used to eat when they was in the war

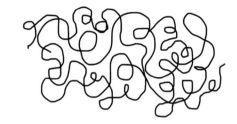

leafs - can be found on most trees and the reason old people like parks is because there is lots of leafs for them to have a eat of

papas very own

Magical
Ground up
Bone Sauce

paste - papas very own magical ground up bone sauce has been voted the most popular ground up bone paste for old people of the past 100 years at the world wide ground up bone awards

exercises for the old:

it is important for old people to keep their body active so that they dont go completely solid and become depressed flesh statues so here is some of the main exercises that a old person can do

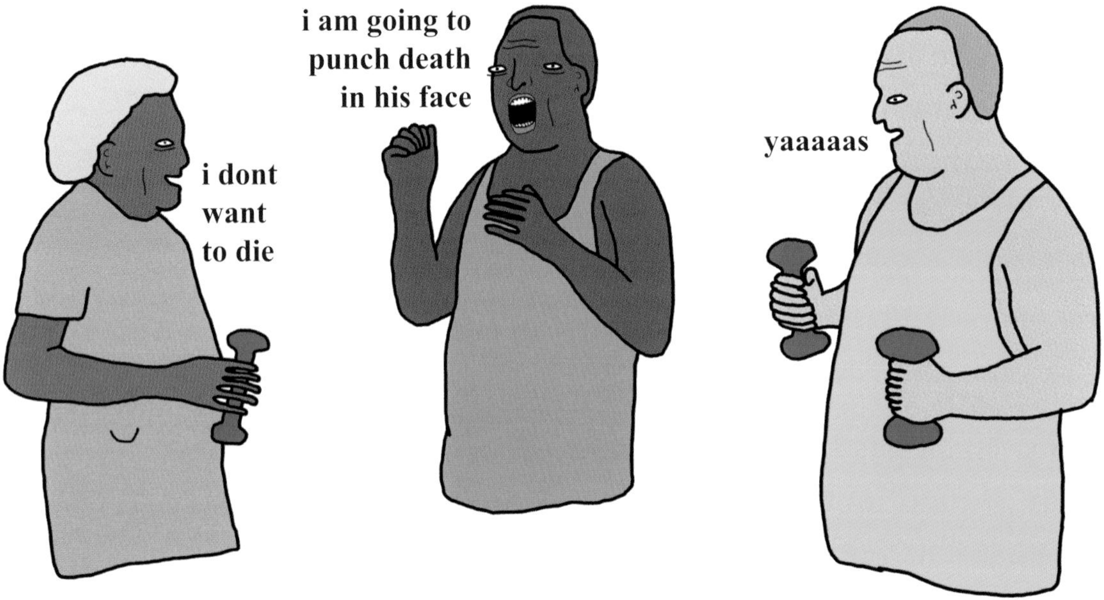
i dont want to die
i am going to punch death in his face
yaaaaas

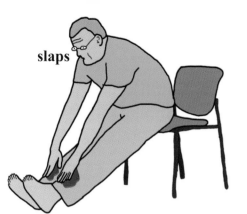

slaps

the leg slap - sit on a chair and slap your legs with your hands until your legs bleed

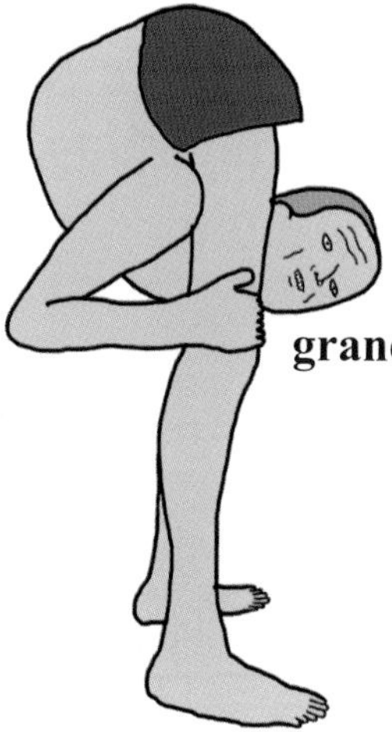

the gentle stretch - gently put your face and most of your head between your legs and scream your own name for as long as you can

grandad

sucks

the plum - stand on your hands like your hands are long toed feet and suck a plum off the ground over and over until the plum has completely dissolved into just its seed

<u>old mens earlobes</u>

old men have really long earlobes that they use to communicate
with each other by flapping them about or stretching them until they bleed
to let other old men know
how they are feeling
without having
to use their
painful
dying
throats

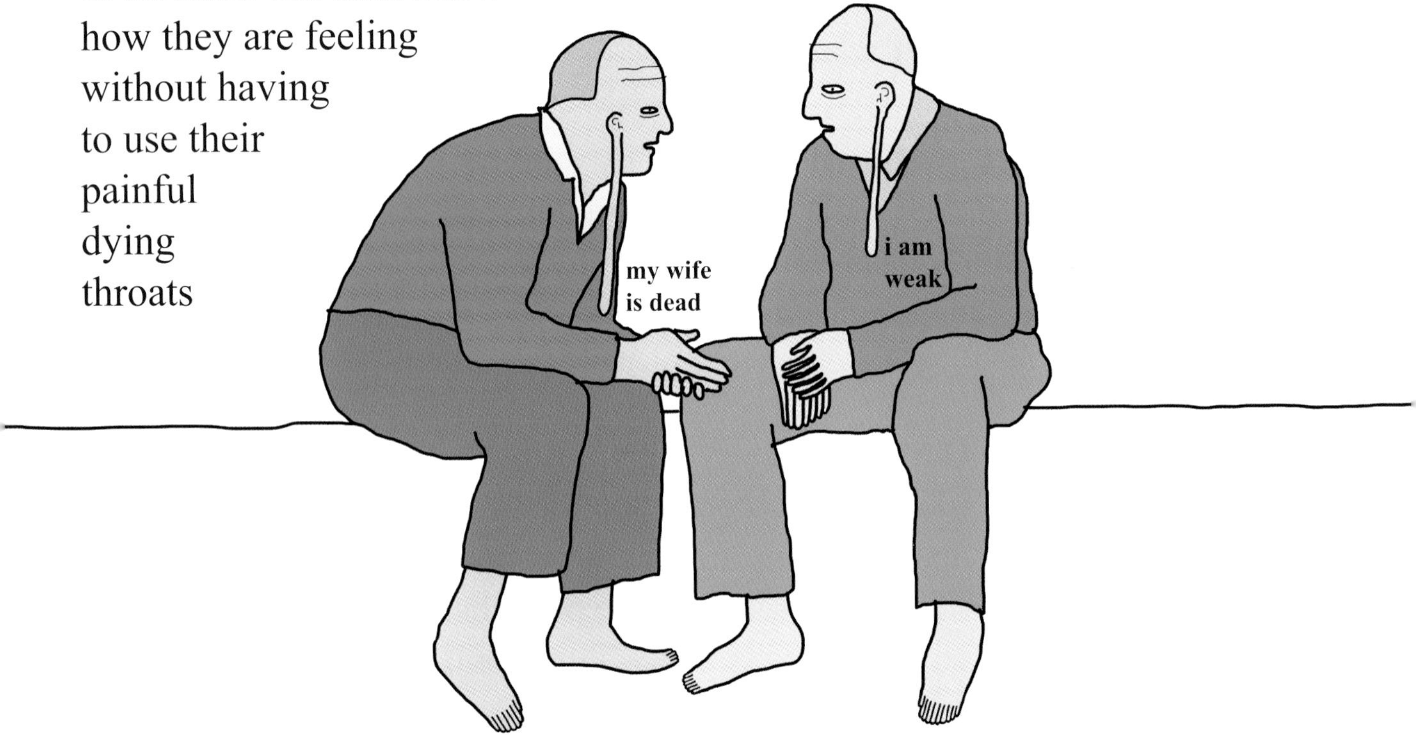
my wife is dead
i am weak

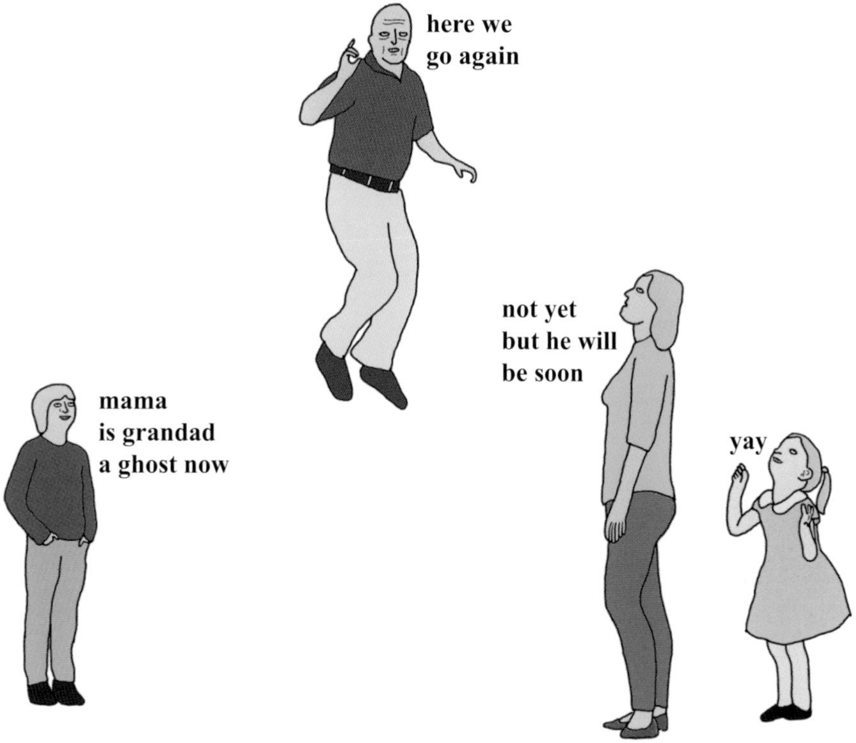
here we go again
mama is grandad a ghost now
not yet but he will be soon
yay

when old people are in the final years of their life
they will start to float for about 3 hours a day
to get them used to becoming a ghost

as the days pass by we start to lose those who were once there by our side

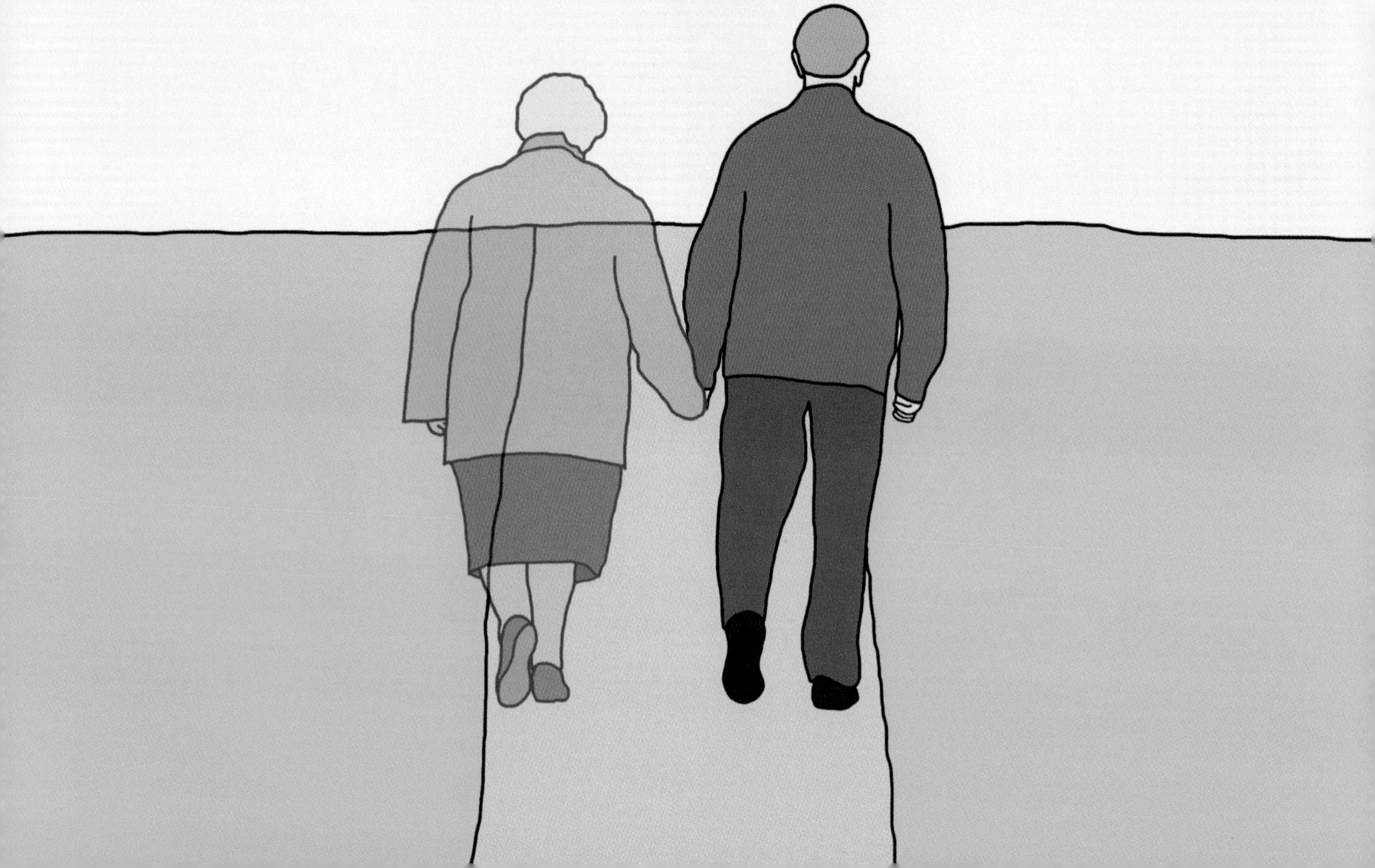

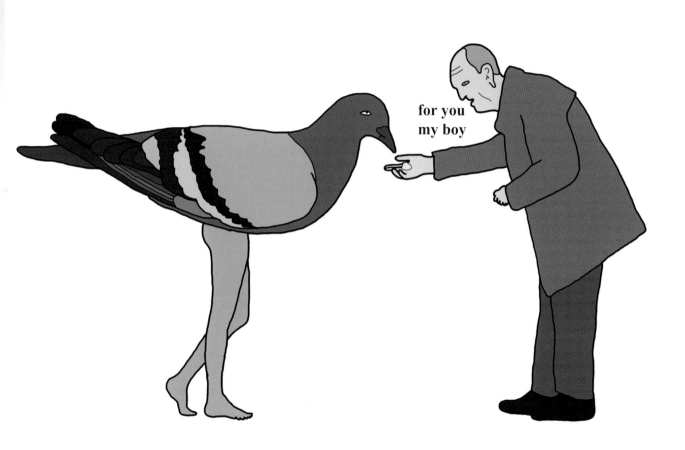

soon it feels like the pigeons are your only friend

goodbye papa
see ya
we will
miss you
i love
you all

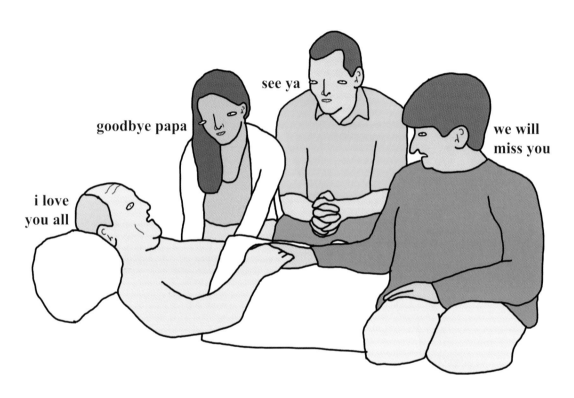

when it is time for you to die your family will come to say goodbye
they will talk about the beautiful life that you have had
and how proud they were that you was their dad

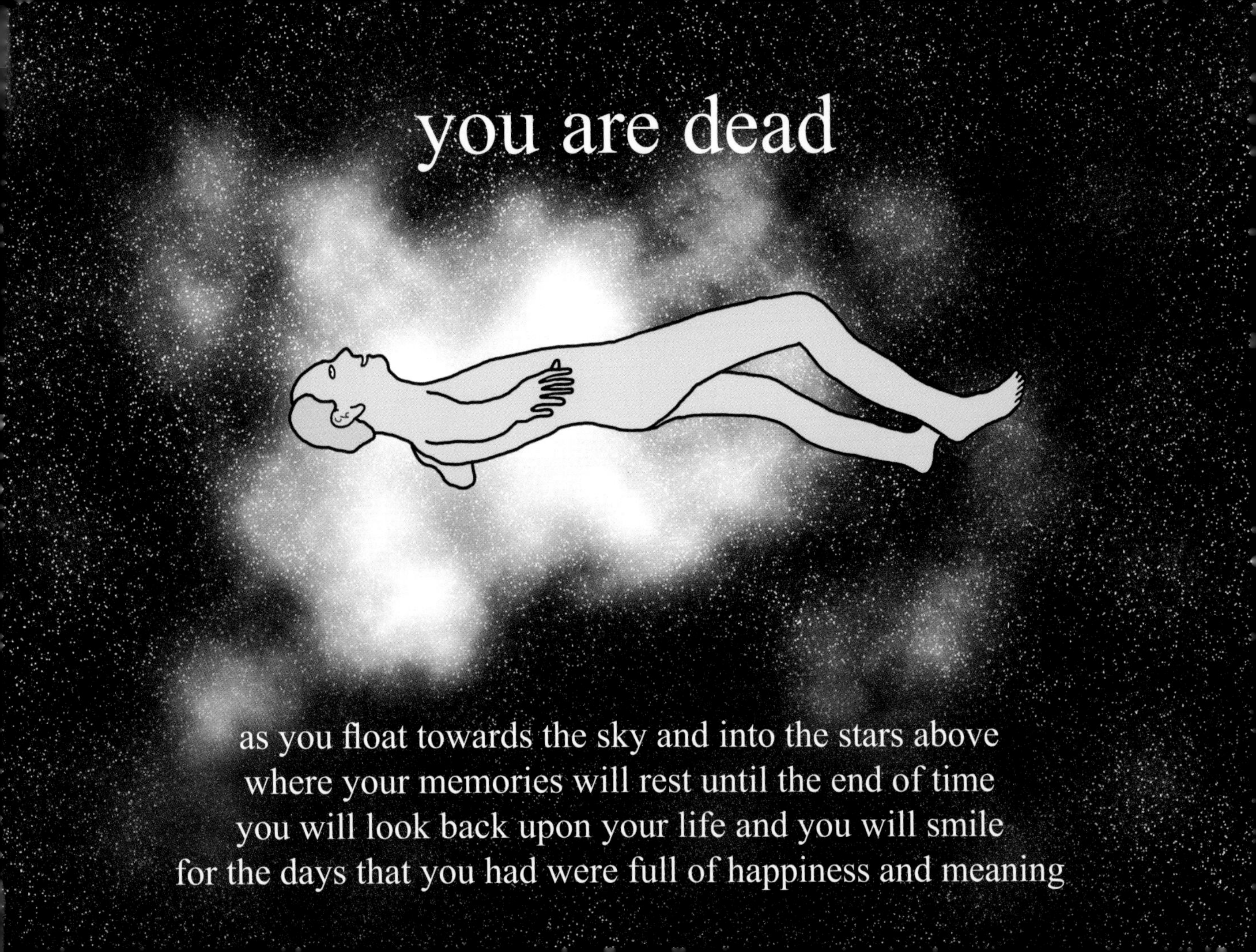
you are dead
as you float towards the sky and into the stars above
where your memories will rest until the end of time
you will look back upon your life and you will smile
for the days that you had were full of happiness and meaning

just because you are dead it doesnt mean that you have to be miserable about it
so here is some fun things to do when you are a ghost:

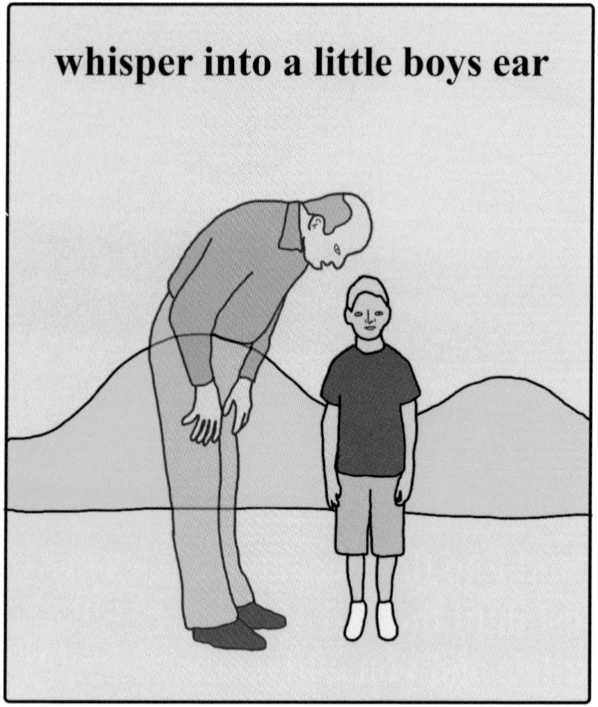
whisper into a little boys ear

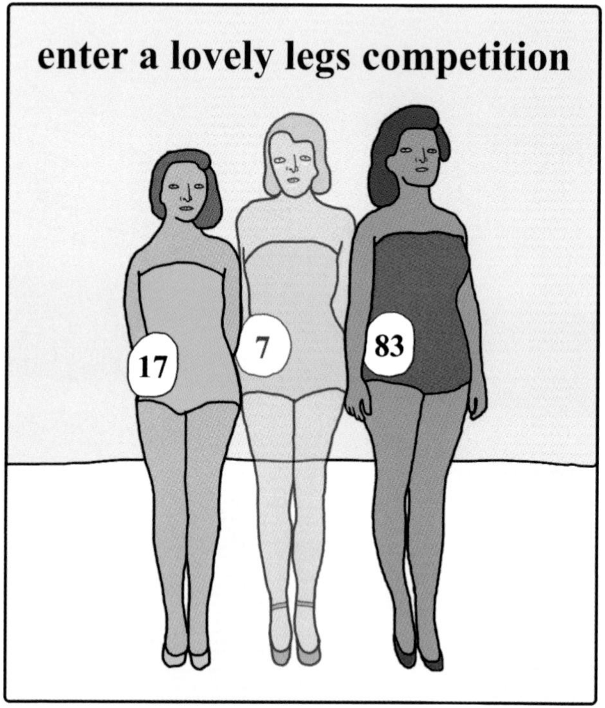
enter a lovely legs competition
17
7
83

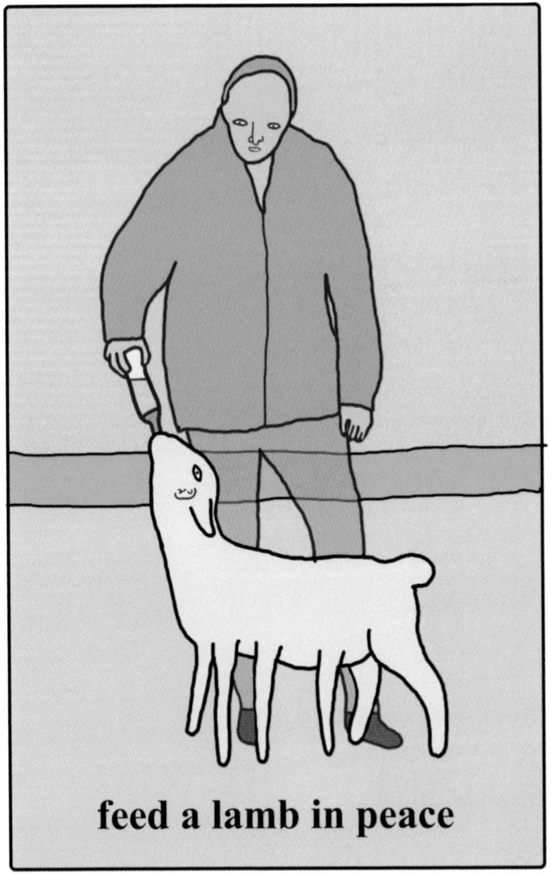
feed a lamb in peace

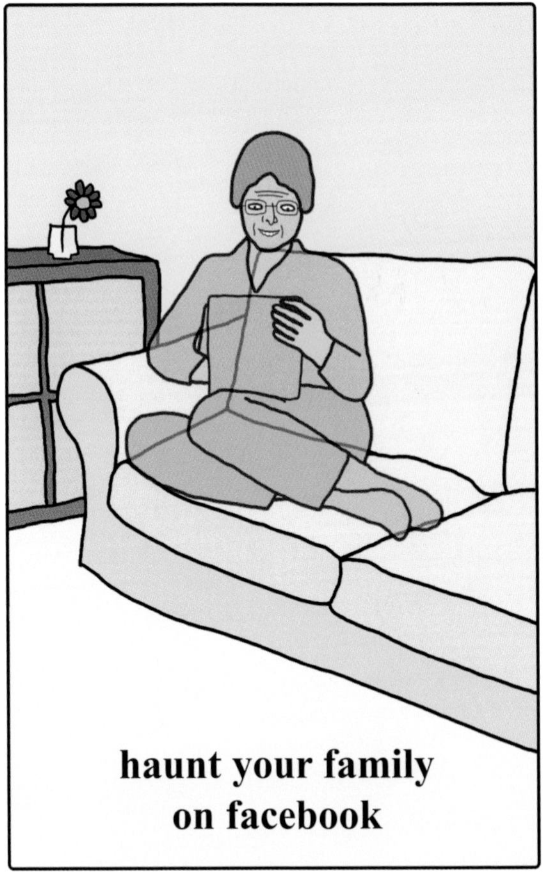
haunt your family
on facebook

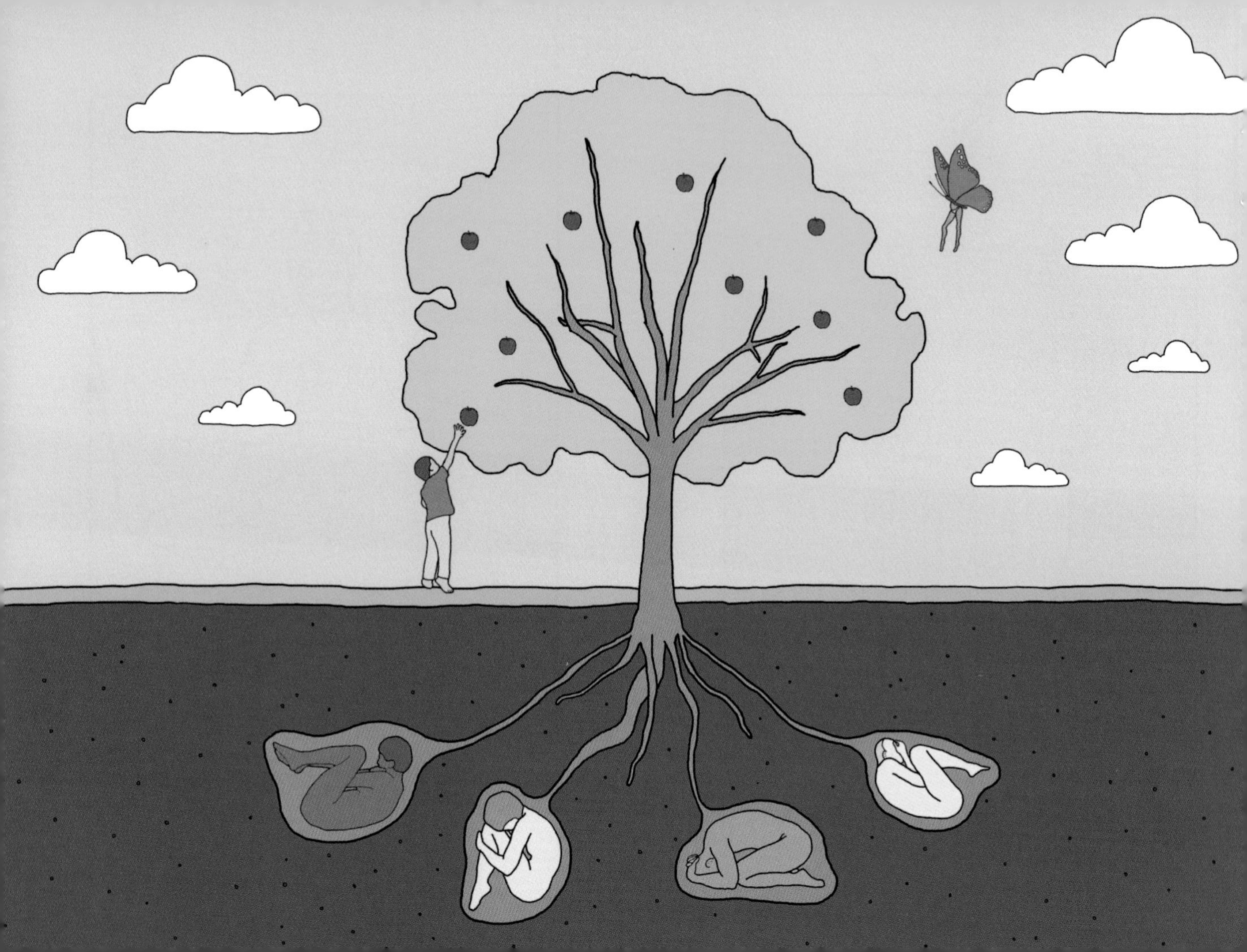

the meaning of life

we are all made of the same things as all around us
like the trees and the fruit and the stars of the universe
we all have the same coloured hearts
that beat in time with the earths own heart too
we wake each day to search for love and for friendship
and for something that will make us feel whole
the search for meaning is different for every person
but the search remains our goal
by giving love to others creates meaning in their own self
and by doing so we create meaning in our own
to smile and to laugh and to cry and to hold
we were young and one day we will be old
we are the universe
and we are time
i am yours
and you are mine

love from your friend Chris (Simpsons artist) xox

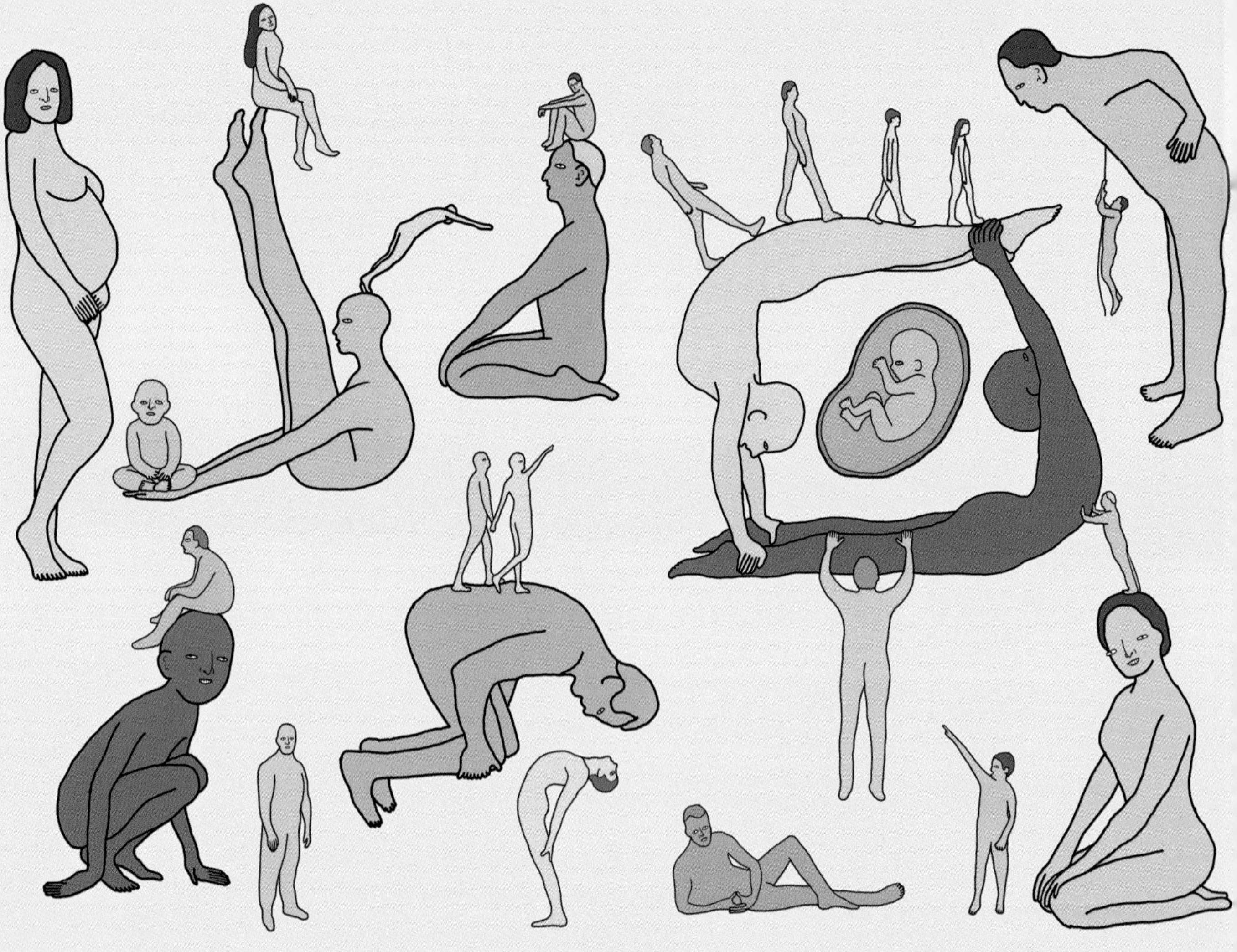